the
petit appetit
COOKBOOK

♥

Easy Organic Recipes to Nurture

Your Baby *and* Toddler

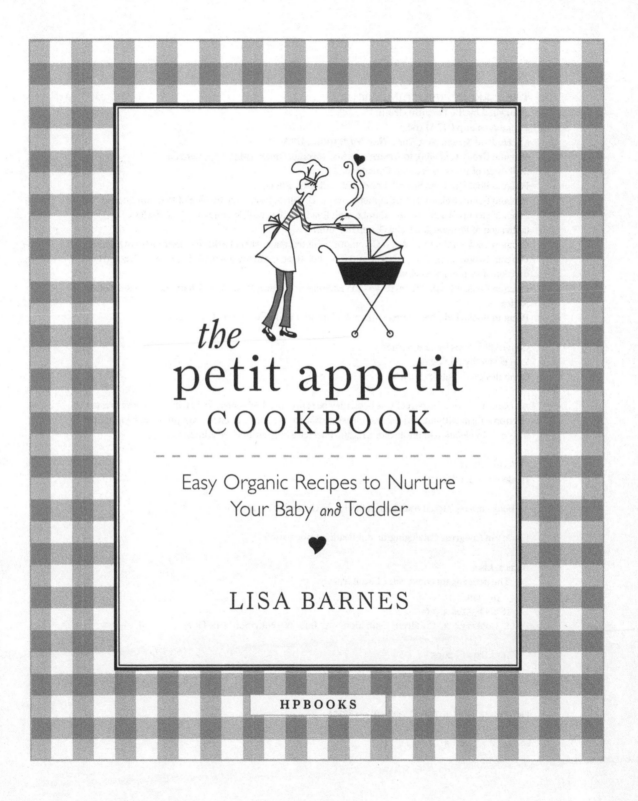

the
petit appetit
COOKBOOK

Easy Organic Recipes to Nurture
Your Baby *and* Toddler

♥

LISA BARNES

HPBOOKS

THE BERKLEY PUBLISHING GROUP
Published by the Penguin Group
Penguin Group (USA) Inc.
375 Hudson Street, New York, New York 10014, USA
Penguin Group (Canada), 10 Alcorn Avenue, Toronto, Ontario M4V 3B2, Canada
(a division of Pearson Penguin Canada Inc.)
Penguin Books Ltd., 80 Strand, London WC2R 0RL, England
Penguin Group Ireland, 25 St. Stephen's Green, Dublin 2, Ireland (a division of Penguin Books Ltd.)
Penguin Group (Australia), 250 Camberwell Road, Camberwell, Victoria 3124, Australia
(a division of Pearson Australia Group Pty. Ltd.)
Penguin Books India Pvt. Ltd., 11 Community Centre, Panchsheel Park, New Delhi—110 017, India
Penguin Group (NZ), Cnr. Airborne and Rosedale Roads, Albany, Auckland 1310, New Zealand (a division of Pearson New Zealand Ltd.)
Penguin Books (South Africa) (Pty.) Ltd., 24 Sturdee Avenue, Rosebank, Johannesburg 2196, South Africa
Penguin Books Ltd., Registered Offices: 80 Strand, London WC2R 0RL, England

Copyright © 2005 by Lisa Barnes
Text design by Jill Weber
Cover design by Satoko Furuta

PRINTING HISTORY
HPBooks / March 2005

HPBooks is a registered trademark of Penguin Group (USA) Inc.

Library of Congress Cataloging-in-Publication Information

Barnes, Lisa.
    The petit appetit cookbook / Lisa Barnes.
        p.   cm.
    ISBN 1-55788-453-6
    1. Cookery.   2. Children—Nutrition.   3. Infants—Nutrition.   I. Title.

  TX652.B3198   2005
  641.5'622—dc22

                                                         2004052300

PRINTED IN THE UNITED STATES OF AMERICA

10   9   8   7   6   5   4   3   2   1

Contents

Acknowledgments

THERE ARE MANY PEOPLE that helped shape this book. I express my gratitude to everyone who contributed, from doctors and nutritionists to restaurateurs and farmers. I am indebted to Sara Duskin, all the parents, and my family and friends for sharing their wisdom and stories.

Through my classes and discussions, I have learned quite a bit from my friends and clients, and their children. Thanks to all of the little taste-testers who gobbled up, spit out, smeared around, and dropped to the floor my test foods, especially Anna, Benjamin, Delilah, Emma, Cole, Jack, Olivia, and Tommy who were there from the beginning bites.

Before, during, and after the children ate, I shoved a spoon into my husband's face at all hours of the day and night and said, "Here, taste!" Thank you, Lee, for always opening your mouth and being so supportive with this venture and everything else I attempt to do. I love you.

While recipe testing I gave birth to my own in-house "official taste-tester." Our son Jonas spent many days in the kitchen watching me cook, and playing with utensils. Someday I hope he'll know how much I appreciated his smile, patience, and palate.

This project took more time and energy than I had anticipated once Jonas arrived. Many thanks for his grandparents' efforts to visit, occupy, and love Jonas while I needed to write and meet deadlines. You didn't need much persuading for the job, but thanks for your generosity and encouragement: Nana (my first "editor" and cheerleader), Poppa, Gido, Aunt Christy (a vegan who only ate bologna and hot dogs when we were growing up), Uncle Craig, Grandma, and Grandpa.

Finally thank you to my agent, Nancy Crossman, for finding my website and making this book a reality, and Jeanette Egan who was a patient editor for this first-time author.

Acknowl-
edgments

♥

Foreword

Just as there is an ethic to growing food, there is also an ethic to eating. . . . Kids have to be taught that fresh, nourishing food is their birthright. . . .

ALICE WATERS, *Chez Panisse*

I TEACH NEW PARENTS, and I have never found a parent who didn't want their child to be smart, sociable, and integrated into their family and community. In this book, Lisa Barnes describes the crucial process by which parents can help their child take the first steps into the world of the family and community. It all begins, not surprisingly, with food. Take two children: The parent of the first hurriedly opens a jar of baby food and spoons it in the child's mouth. The second child is in the kitchen and experiences the washing, chopping, tasting, mixing, and cooking. Which child learns more? Can any TV or Internet experience compare with the sensory and intellectual experience of witnessing the whole process of food preparation and consumption?

Lisa shows that it's even more than that. At the same time the child is learning, the parents are learning to make healthy choices. They understand the value of organic foods and are warned to read the labels of processed foods. Lisa shows it doesn't have to be a lot of extra work but that it's fun and productive to help your baby develop while preparing organic foods that the whole family will enjoy eating. Why not, for example, make a bean puree for baby and bean soup for the rest of the family?

Lisa has produced a road map showing when the child is ready to move on to new foods, how the parents can easily prepare healthy meals, and how to shop for and identify good organic food for each stage of the child's development, so the baby can safely reach the goal of eating the family meal as soon as he or she is developmentally ready. I will recommend this book in my teaching as a health educator and lactation consultant.

SARA U. DUSKIN, Health Educator, C.L.E., I.B.C.L.C

Introduction

I always wondered why babies spend so much time sucking their thumbs. Then I tasted baby food.

ROBERT ORBEN, American humorist

L IVING IN SAN FRANCISCO, a city so rich in culinary culture, I wondered why so many children were eating strange-colored, mass-produced food from a jar. I thought this wasn't fair, and felt guilty that as an adult I was entitled to good, fresh food, but the children I knew were eating frozen and processed foods. I knew there must be alternatives.

Every year parents in the United States spend $3.9 billion on baby food. The big baby food manufacturers have built their names on convenience and marketing, but not on taste, quality, and nutrition. In Northern California we have access to all the freshest foods year-round from farmer's markets, local growers, organic specialty stores, and more than four thousand restaurants.

One night my husband and I were headed out with friends to the latest culinary hot spot. Before our friends could leave, they needed to feed their son, finish getting dressed (or redressed if the feeding was too messy), and give instructions to the babysitter. My friend, a usually calm mother was shoveling gray peas at her sweet baby, while he squirmed and cried over the forced-food experience. What, I wondered, had happened to the family meal and "comfort foods"? Cooking and eating is a sign of affection and social interaction. Jarred carrots, boxed macaroni and cheese, and packaged Happy Meals can't be the answer.

Later, while attending a baby shower, I heard all of the expectant moms say they were going to make their own baby food. They had the best intentions but months later when the babies were ready to eat solids, the mothers said they were too scared to make their children's food, or never had time to learn to cook. Who could blame them? Feeding a baby was a new experience, and it was easier to buy the "trusted" big names in baby food, even though these parents knew that wasn't the healthiest or tastiest option. Because I've always loved to cook (and eat) and took cooking classes in my spare time, I decided to make homemade, fresh baby food and give it to new moms for gifts.

My friends joked about "that movie from the eighties with Diane Keaton." They could never remember the name, until one day my mom called and said, "*Baby Boom.*" I rented it and I identified. Diane Keaton went from being an urban, high-powered executive to a suburban mother and applesauce entrepreneur. Why weren't the big companies making fresh baby foods? Where were the Diane Keatons of the world? I began doing lots of research, discovering what's in jarred foods, who markets these foods, what children like to eat, how eating habits are created, and the significance of bringing the family together at mealtimes.

When I started my business, Petit Appetit, all of my energy was focused on preparing healthy and tasty food. I was teaching parents how to cook, making toddler snacks and meals, shopping for produce, meeting with dietitians and nutritionists, taking more cooking classes, recipe testing, and becoming a safe food handler. Then I began reading and researching about the state of children's health in America, which was overwhelming: the rise in juvenile diabetes, the increase of childhood obesity, the potential danger in pesticides and preservatives, the money spent on junk and fast foods, the lack of whole foods in children's diets, and the reduction in childhood exercise, just to name a few of the issues.

I realized children's good eating habits aren't just a need in a "foodie" city like San Francisco. Every parent wants to provide the best food possible for his or her children. While teaching Bay Area parents to prepare baby foods, I realized that parents living everywhere would benefit from these lessons. A few clients thought the recipes were so great, they asked me if I could ship my fresh baby foods to their girlfriends in other cities and states. My small business was not going to meet the demand.

I decided that writing a cookbook is the best way to share what I've learned from clients, parents, children, and experts. While writing this book, I had my most important client, my son, Jonas. Of course I thought because of my ongoing research and work cooking for children, I would be completely prepared to feed Jonas. I had questions, too! If having a child teaches us anything, it is that each child is unique and special, and may not do, eat, or say what you anticipate by researching and studying. Jonas's culinary adventure has been a good journey so far. Hopefully the information shared here will guide you and your child to make the experience of eating and cooking as enjoyable and fulfilling as possible, and that the food choices and habits you create work best for your individual family. This book will provide you with an alternative to buying commercially processed foods, and enable you to trust your own cooking and parenting abilities. You can then feel confident to create healthy menus, adventurous palates, and positive eating habits for your children.

I still love to watch a child eat their first bite of something they've never tasted. I find it amazing that one minute a child has no reference for the taste and texture of a food and then a mouthful later they are reaching for the spoon, making happy faces, wearing it as a badge of honor, and even asking you to make it again. This is a tremendous reward. Making your own food isn't for everyone, every day of the week. However, knowing you can create healthy options and choices for your child, which fit your lifestyle and provide a nourishing and socially positive mealtime, is invaluable.

Bon Petit Appetit!

the
petit appetit
COOKBOOK
♥
Easy Organic Recipes to Nurture
Your Baby *and* Toddler

Chapter 1

Using This Book

YOU ARE READING THIS BOOK because your child's eating habits, nutrition, and palate are important to you. This book will help you navigate your child's nutritional needs and culinary adventure from birth to four years and beyond. The goal is to have a healthy family who likes to share, socialize, and celebrate together over mealtimes for years to come.

The first step to getting the most out of this book is to identify the developmental stage of your child. The developmental stage is of greater importance than age, because each child develops different motor skills and interests at a different rate. The ages mentioned for each group is only a guide and a guess as to how old your child might be at these developmental stages. Your child may start his culinary adventure at four and a half months, while your sister's baby may not be eating until seven months; you both would start at The Beginners (page 54). The one who started earlier will progress to the next stage, The Explorers (page 76), sooner because he's had more experience, textures, and flavors. But they'll both be on their way and setting their own pace. Food and eating is not a competition. If your baby is not ready to begin solids, do not push him. Alternatively, if your baby shows a real interest in your food, do not deny trying solids. Feeding should not be a frightening process.

Even when beginning solids it is recommended that you continue

THE CULINARY ADVENTURE:

THE BEGINNERS 4 to 6 Months	THE EXPLORERS 6 to 9 Months	THE INDEPENDENTS 9 to 12 Months
Recipes Chapter 7	Recipes Chapter 8	Recipes Chapter 9
Holds head up when sitting Follows food with eyes Opens mouth for spoon Begins to swallow solids Loses tongue thrust reflex	Sits up in highchair without support Closes lips over spoon Palms food and scrapes food from hand to mouth Keeps food in mouth and munches up and down Cutting teeth Has tried a variety of single-ingredient foods	Wants to hold spoon and feed himself Chews with rotary motion Move from palming hand to pincer grasp (thumb and forefinger) Can drink from a "sip" cup Has food favorites

feeding breast milk or formula through the first year, because that is still where babies receive most of the vitamins and minerals needed for growth and development. There are some telltale signs that your baby is ready to eat solids and when to advance to different foods and textures. Review the following chart to see where your baby is now, and when to begin their culinary adventure.

The stages, while identified, are not meant to be an excuse for you to stop providing a healthy and positive eating environment for your child. As an example, some children become very active at the Movers and Shakers stages (pages 134 and 170). This does not mean they should now be allowed to eat while playing, or be excused from the usual family mealtime. The earlier you establish the mealtime expectations and schedule, the more likely everyone will stick to the routine.

About the Chapters

The first six chapters of this book will teach you the benefits of preparing your own food, nutrition and health needs, shopping tips, the importance of organics, and how to set up a safe kitchen. If you're introducing solids for the first time, you'll

Stages and Developmental Signs

| THE MOVERS | THE SHAKERS | THE CONNOISSEURS |
12 to 24 Months	2 to 3 Years	3 to 4 Years
Recipes Chapter 10	Recipes Chapter 11	Recipes Chapter 12
Picking up finger foods	Interest in cooking and kitchen	Wants to help in kitchen and participate in mealtimes
Improving chewing and controlling food in mouth	Asking for specific foods	Mimics your table manners and eating habits
Drinking well from cup	Exercising will at mealtimes	More adept at using utensils
	May not want to sit still to eat	
	Learning about foods, colors, where food comes from	
	May refuse past favorite foods	

want to read Chapter 3, which explains how to monitor new foods and check for signs of food allergies and intolerances. Before trying any of the recipes, read Chapter 5 for helpful reminders about kitchen safety and safe food handling practices. If you are confused (and most of us are) about organic food labels and buzzwords such as "grass-fed beef," read Chapter 6 to understand what you are and aren't buying. And for tips on making mealtimes and cooking fun and educational, see Chapter 4. These first chapters will help you at all stages of your child's culinary adventure, and should be referenced as needed.

Chapters 7 through 12 are the recipes. Each chapter is dedicated to a developmental stage with a description of what to expect for a healthy child's diet and eating habits. Keep in mind that your child is an individual and you will learn his own appetite and eating habits, which may not match the descriptions exactly. For instance, parents always ask how much their child should be eating. According to nutritionist Mary Ellen DiPaola, it is really up to each child. Therefore, look at the amounts (taken from the American Pediatric Association) only as a guide. As long as your child is growing and thriving, you can let your child dictate his own appetite.

About the Recipes

Once you know which foods are appropriate for your child and you're confident to start cooking, read the recipes. The recipes have been reviewed by parents and nutritionists to find a balance of appetizing meals that are also quick and easy to prepare. Some do not even need a microwave. Each recipe shows the ingredients, amounts, nutritional analysis, prep tips, and ingredient icons. To simplify your life and your trips to the supermarket, check out the Stocking the Kitchen tips (page 13). The idea is to make cooking for your family easy, so use alternative ingredients (sometimes given in the recipe tips), and feel free to add ingredients to improve the recipe to suit your family's tastes. If your child's health professional has diagnosed your child with allergies, intolerances, or health issues, the recipe icons can help quickly identify recipes that meet dietary and cooking restrictions. See the index for a list of the recipes that fit into the different categories.

Recipe Icons and Definitions

 Egg-free: Recipes without eggs, especially for those with egg allergies and adults with cholesterol concerns.

 Gluten-free: Recipes without gluten, which is found mostly in wheat, but also in some other grains in small amounts. Recipes use gluten-free alternative flours and grains, especially convenient for those with celiac disease (see Chapter 3, page 23 for definition).

 No Cook: Simple recipes that do not need to be cooked, even in a microwave, for when parents need quick and easy food ideas.

 No Sugar Added: Recipes without added sugar or sweetener such as brown rice syrup and molasses.

 Wheat-free: Recipes without wheat (see gluten-free above), especially for babies with wheat allergies.

Vegetarian: Recipes without animal meats, including poultry and fish, but may contain eggs or milk products.

Vegan: Recipes without any animal products, including honey, eggs, or dairy products.

Nutritional Analysis

The analyses of the recipes were performed by CompuFood Analysis, Inc. Some things to note:

- When the ingredient, sauce, or serving suggestions is optional or not included in the main recipe, it is not included in the nutritional analysis.

- The serving sizes are based on the Food and Drug Administration portions for adults for many of the recipes. However, the Beginners' and Explorers' recipes, such as the purees, are based on an average baby serving.

Ingredients

Please note that although the recipes will list organically grown and raised produce and meat, conventionally grown and raised ingredients will work as well. Although grocery stores are expanding their inventory of natural and organic foods, some ingredients may not be readily available at your local supermarket. Expeller pressed canola oil may be readily available in San Francisco, but not easy to find in Plains, Montana. You can check local specialty stores, health food stores, or online (see the store and Web site resources on page 255), or substitute with another item. In this case, regular canola oil would be fine. Recipes will make note of such ingredients and substitutions.

Getting Started

Once you've got your ingredients and have chosen a recipe, start cooking! If your dish comes out as expected, great! If not, that's okay, too. What's the worst that can happen? You've overcooked the peas, and they're mushy? Try it again, and watch the temperature and timing more closely. These recipes are meant to empower you, not intimidate you. The food will taste great because the ingredients are simple and fresh, not because they are fancy, hard to pronounce, or need the skills of a four-star chef. Do not be discouraged if your child does not eat your food right away. According to nutritionists, babies may need to be introduced to a food up to fifteen times before they eat it. So keep trying and eventually they'll appreciate the color, taste, and texture. Keep in mind this experience is new for everyone, so be patient and have fun.

> The information contained in this book should not be used as a substitute for the medical care and nutritional advice of your pediatrician. There may be variations in treatment and diet that your pediatrician may recommend based upon your child's individual needs, health, and circumstances.

Chapter 2

Creating Convenience

MAKING YOUR OWN BABY FOOD has to work for you and your lifestyle. The idea is to make cooking easy, so here are some ways to help you save time, effort, and money when shopping, cooking, and eating.

To Market, To Market . . .

You've probably heard this before but the easiest and healthiest way to shop at the supermarket is to stay mainly on the perimeter of the store. This is where you'll find the fresh and whole foods, such as the meat, fish, and poultry departments, the fruits and vegetables, and the dairy, fresh juices, and eggs. Eating whole foods is the most important thing to remember when feeding your family. In contrast, when you stroll down the center aisles you'll find the canned and frozen foods, processed snacks, and sugary beverages.

While I suggest taking your child to the grocery store to get them involved, I do know what a challenge this can be. If you are prepared with a list, you'll be more focused and less likely to forget those important staple items. You may even want to create one list of everyday items that you can make copies of to always have ready for each trip to the store. Then all you need to do is add or delete as necessary, rather than re-create the list each time. See tips on Stocking the Kitchen (page 13).

Labels

When choosing groceries, read the labels until you establish the foods and brands that you want to continue buying for your family. This may take time at first and is tough to do with a toddler in tow. Reading labels can save you time and money in the long run, as well as avoid foods that may pose a health risk to your family. There are so many options for each type of food that you'll want to compare to get the best value and nutrition. Don't be lead by the big names you're bombarded with by television commercials. The leading brand of toasted oats cereal not only has additives, preservatives, and more sugar than the organic version, but also costs more!

Here are a few things to keep in mind when reading labels:

- The ingredients are listed in order of amount, largest to smallest. Thus a cereal listing sugar as the first ingredient has more sugar compared to other ingredients than another cereal listing sugar last.

- If you don't recognize and can't pronounce items listed on the ingredients label, those are most likely preservatives and additives that you and your family are better off without.

- There are hidden trans fats and sugars disguised under names such as partially hydrogenated oil and corn syrup.

- Don't be fooled by food labeled "for children." Juice is the same whether it says it's for kids or not. You should look for "100% juice" on the label, not a slick label with a happy child on the container. Often the regular version is less expensive than that directed at the "kids' market."

- Do not assume that because a food is labeled "for children" it is safe and healthy. There are many trans fats and chemicals in food for children. Even zwieback teething biscuits have additives, preservatives, and partially hydrogenated oils.

Jarred Baby Foods: What You Are Buying

In America, a parent puts food in front of a child and says, "Eat it, it's good for you."
In Europe, the parent says, "Eat it. It's good!"

JOHN LEVEE in *Another Way of Living*, by John Bainbridge

Four million babies are born in the United States every year. By the time they reach twelve months of age, each of those infants has consumed, smeared around, or spit out an average of six hundred jars of baby food. By contrast, the average baby born in Western Europe will consume only about 240 jars of baby food, and in Eastern European countries, like Poland, about twelve jars, according to Dr. Michael Jacobson of the Center for Science in the Public Interest.

Americans have long depended on jarred baby foods for convenience. In the past few years more and more processed food options have entered the children's food market. The big brands have expanded into prepackaged "toddler meals" and "school lunches" all in the name of helping busy parents who need things to be fast and convenient. Even for those parents with the best intentions, there may be times when you just can't make or safely pack your own food. One of my clients had served her eight-month-old homemade, organic baby food from his first bite. However while traveling with her son to England, she brought a few jars of food "just in case" she ran out of fresh items on the flight.

Here are some tips for buying commercially jarred foods, when you're in a pinch.

- ◆ Choose those with the most calories, meaning more food per unit weight.

- ◆ Look for jars of organic foods, without fillers.

- ◆ Check that the expiration date on the jar has not passed.

- ◆ Choose foods without chemicals and preservatives.

- ◆ If feeding your baby a vegetarian diet, look for the Vegetarian Society's "V" symbol on the jar or container, to be sure it is truly vegetarian.

- ◆ Make sure the vacuum seal button on the lid is down.

Benefits of Homemade

Babies usually triple their weight during their first year. If they are what they eat, this is the most important time to give them the best. You may not be able to give your child fresh, homemade foods every day, but there are benefits for you and your child when you do make the effort.

MORE NUTRITIOUS

Homemade food is more nutritious than commercially prepared baby foods because it retains more of the nutrients, especially the B vitamins and vitamin C. This is because the food is less processed. The jarring process necessitates the use of very high heat under pressure, much more than you can generate when cooking at home. Unfortunately, many vitamins are destroyed by heat.

Some of the baby food on the market has additives and thickening agents, including cornstarch, flour, chemically modified starches, or tapioca. This means your baby is getting less fruit and vegetables and more "filler." Your baby is also getting less nutrition and value for the money.

MORE CONTROL

By making your own food, you'll know exactly what your child is eating. You can monitor his diet, and know which vitamins and nutrients are lacking. A study by the *San Francisco Chronicle* in 2002 reported that over 40 percent of children's calories come from fast and processed foods. Spend your time making your own food, rather than reading and decoding labels on processed foods.

NO CHEMICALS OR PRESERVATIVES

Your food will not have anything added, that you didn't put there. You're not trying to preserve shelf life or disguise any of the ingredients in your food. Preservatives include partially hydrogenated oils or trans fats, which are linked to diabetes, cancer, and heart disease.

TASTE

While sometimes convenient, a big drawback of commercial baby food is that it bears little relation to the real food. Fresh, seasonal food just tastes better. You probably haven't eaten baby food since you were a baby, because you don't want or have to. If you feed your baby homemade baby food, your child will appreciate real foods from his first bite. These will be the same flavors and foods that he will continue to enjoy as he grows. Jarred baby food is not available in every fruit and vegetable, nor is it seasonal. You may miss the opportunity to introduce fruit and vegetable options, which you want your baby to eat later with the rest of the family. Some children get used to bland, smooth, jarred foods and have difficulty being reintroduced to the same real foods and textures later.

LESS WASTE

Making food gives you control over quantity, taste, texture, and expense. You will not have to throw away partially eaten jars of food. Instead you can cook what you know your baby will eat, prolong the life of your homemade food in the freezer, or eat your child's leftover food yourself.

You can use a single, whole food item in different ways. When you bake sweet potatoes you can chose to puree some, cut pieces into soft chunks, and leave the rest whole. Because your homemade purees are made with whole foods, the leftovers can be made into soups, side dishes, and sauces for the rest of the family. You may doubt that because you've never considered making a delicious soup from a jar of baby food. However my family's favorite butternut squash soup starts with leftover, fresh puree for baby (see recipe page 63).

> *It never even occurred to me to buy jarred baby food for my son. My husband and I didn't eat jarred or canned foods, so why give them to him? My son is now a healthy fourteen-year-old who continues to eat fresh foods and try new things with the rest of our family.*
>
> GLENDA HAMILTON, Newborn Connections,
> California Pacific Medical Center

LESS COST

The cost for making your own baby food is often less than buying commercially prepared baby foods, if you shop smart and cook in larger quantities. For instance a 4-ounce jar of baby food ranges in price from 60 cents to $1.20 each, depending on brand and place purchased. However, when making your own baby food and following our tips for creating convenience and buying in-season whole foods, you can save on the price. I purchased enough apples for the Apple Puree (page 59) for $2.00 at the farmers' market, and my recipe yielded 16 ounces; thus my cost was 50 cents per 4-ounce serving.

PLANNING AHEAD: THINKING BEFORE COOKING

Having healthy food choices at home keeps you from running out for takeout or high-priced prepared foods. You can create your own version of fast foods if you plan ahead. Besides stocking the pantry, here are a few other suggestions:

◆ Make large amounts of fruit and veggie purees for baby. If baby doesn't eat them or you discover an allergy, you can easily make great soups, sauces, and sides for the other family members.

◆ Freeze baby food, adult sauces, and cooking broths in ice-cube containers. Once frozen, pop them out and seal in plastic freezer bags labeled with the food item and date. You can thaw and use them anytime.

◆ Make extra portions when you cook, so you can freeze leftovers.

◆ Cook once for the whole week, but create variety by reinventing the main ingredient for new meals. If you cook one or two whole chickens on Sunday, you can use the leftovers later in the week to make salads, pasta, tacos, and sandwiches.

> *The most remarkable thing about my mother is that for thirty years she served the family nothing but leftovers. The original meal has never been found.*
>
> CALVIN TRILLIN

Stocking the Kitchen

A food processor? Oh, maybe we do have one. We have some kitchen stuff we've never unpacked from our wedding three years ago.

SEVEN-MONTH-OLD COLE'S mom

A well-stocked kitchen is the foundation for preparing convenient and healthy meals at home. The right equipment and cooking tools allow you to cook and store foods easily. A well-stocked pantry and refrigerator means never having to run out of the house for last-minute ingredients or takeout foods.

Many cookbooks and baby books tell you to go out and buy specific equipment to prepare your baby's food. I've had clients spend money on food mills and baby food grinders only to be disappointed by the prices and functionality. Your baby's food can be made with kitchen appliances and tools you probably already have. The easiest way to process food smoothly and efficiently is with a food processor, and that is what I've used in my instructions for purees. This does not mean a special baby food processor, just the regular size, fitted with a steel blade. If you don't have a processor, a blender can substitute.

FEEDING UTENSILS

In the beginning your child does not need fancy china or special dishes. I fed my son out of ramekins, because they were small and I had lots of them. When your baby starts self-feeding you can put food in small plastic bowls or directly onto a highchair tray, for less mess.

What is important to have is special rubber- or plastic-tipped spoons. Your baby's Tiffany spoon is beautiful and fun for baby to bang, but a rubber-tipped spoon is easier on baby's new teeth and sensitive gums. Some of the plastic and rubber baby spoons even change color to warn that food is too hot.

Suggested Equipment and Tools

COOKING

◆ Multilayer steamer pot or steamer basket and cooking pot with lid

◆ Small to medium pan with lid

◆ Baking sheet

◆ Glass baking dish

PREPARING

◆ Food processor, moulis, or baby food mill/grinder

◆ Colored plastic cutting boards or separate wooden boards for each food type (meat, fish, poultry, fruits, and vegetables)

◆ Vegetable peeler

◆ Vegetable brush

◆ Vegetable wash or mild soap

◆ Tongs

◆ Rubber spatula

STORING

◆ Plastic storage containers with lids

◆ Self-sealing plastic freezer and storage bags

◆ Ice cube trays with covers

◆ Black permanent marker

Suggested Foods

REFRIGERATED CONVENIENCE ITEMS

These foods are perishable, and thus must be restocked. Check freshness labels and dates before eating. See page 41 for Food Storage.

Precooked chicken and meats. Already grilled or steamed and ready to add to pasta, salads, stews, stir-fries, fajitas, or to just eat plain.

Precut vegetables and fruits. Vegetables for stir-fries and pastas and fruits for snacking, salads, or smoothies.

Fresh dips and salsas. Use to spice up sandwiches, raw vegetables, crackers, pasta, and baked potatoes.

Pizza and bread dough. Let each family member create his own meal with lots of healthy topping options.

Yogurt. Plain yogurt, which you can add your own fruit and purees to, is particularly important to have on hand. For those under one year, be sure the yogurt is made from whole milk and active cultures. Soy yogurt is an option for those who are lactose intolerant. Plain yogurt is also a good base for salad dressings, smoothies, sauces, and a healthy alternative to sour cream for topping baked potatoes and Mexican foods.

Milk. You may have a few different types of milk (whole, low-fat, and nonfat) for family members based on age and diet. Soy and rice milk are also good alternatives, especially for those with allergies and lactose intolerance. Have on hand for drinking, making smoothies, and baking.

Cheeses. Soft cream cheese makes great dips and spreads for all ages. Adding calcium to your family's diet is as easy as sprinkling fresh Parmesan cheese over pastas and vegetables. Cheddar cheese is always welcome for sandwiches and homemade macaroni and cheese. Soft cheeses such as ricotta and goat cheeses can be a healthy meal or snack spread on crackers or toast. Shredded cheeses are a great way to save time when making your favorite Italian and Mexican dishes.

Eggs. Eggs can be the basis of quick meals by themselves, omelets, egg salad, and quiches. Some kids think "breakfast for dinner" is a fun family meal.

Breads. Breads such as pita, multigrain, lavosh, bagels, and tortillas allow for various stuffings and presentations. Create healthy pizzas, burritos, wraps, sandwiches, and more.

FREEZER ITEMS

Fresh is usually best for taste and nutrients; however, frozen can be a convenient standby. Peas, soybeans, and blueberries make convenient finger foods for older babies and toddlers. Frozen fruit and berries are always ready for smoothies and shakes. Frozen poultry, fish, and meats will enable you to create all kinds of meals.

Don't forget to use your freezer for your homemade leftovers and storage to create your own "convenience" items. Baby's purees, as well as soups, broths, and sauces freeze beautifully in ice cube trays. Make a double batch of cookies or muffins and freeze some in freezer bags for unexpected guests and anytime treats. Most food items can remain in the freezer for up to three months.

PANTRY ITEMS: NONPERISHABLE

Pasta. This can be any shape or size, so you're ready to make spaghetti, lasagna, macaroni and cheese, udon, and soups. Best choices are eggless noodles for those under twelve months and wheat semolina for those over twelve months.

Dried grains. Couscous, quinoa, risotto, and polenta make good side dishes to meats and fish dishes as well as appropriate main dishes with steamed vegetables or stews. They are good staples for Indian and Mediterranean dishes.

Beans and legumes. These include lentils, red kidney beans, garbanzo beans, black beans, and white beans. You'll be prepared for healthy dips such as hummus and black bean, as well as side dishes, soups, and salads.

Rice: Have infant rice on hand for baby's first meals and to mix in with vegetable and fruit purees. Brown rice makes a good and healthy companion for Asian stir-fries and Mexican dishes.

Dried fruits. These are great healthy snacks alone, as well as good mix-ins for yogurt, granola, oatmeal, and cottage cheese.

Breakfast cereals. These include muesli, granola, low-sugar cereals, oat bran, wheat germ, and oatmeal. It's also easy to make your own cereal mix by simply combining your favorite grains such as rolled oats, toasted wheat germ, and oat bran with dried fruit.

CANNED AND JARRED FOODS

Some canned foods are high in fat, sodium, and sugar, but many are also high in nutritional value and are convenient for favorite recipes. Check the labels to identify those with the least additives. These include: light tuna in water, natural organic nut butters, all-fruit spread, beans, tomatoes (especially Pomi brand), and corn. Be sure to drain and thoroughly rinse canned foods to eliminate extra sodium and oils. Keep low-sodium broths and stocks on hand for poaching and boiling meats and vegetables, as well as creating your own soups.

CONDIMENTS

A good supply of bottled sauces, condiments, oils, herbs, and spices will allow for lots of creativity. Ingredients such as naturally brewed soy sauce (tamari), mustards, ketchup, salad dressings, tomato paste, and Worcestershire sauce give flavor to dishes as well as create many dips and sandwich spread options. Use healthy oils such as olive and canola for cooking and baking as well as preparing dressings and marinades. Vinegars such as balsamic are also a good way to add flavor. Check labels once items are open for proper refrigeration and storage.

Herbs and spices are best when fresh, but even dried can wake up a boring food. Dried does not mean old. As spices age, they loose their flavor. If possible buy whole herbs and spices and grind them yourself (a clean coffee grinder works well) for maximum taste.

Chapter 3

Meeting the Needs: Health, Palate, and Lifestyle

Nutrients

More and more studies are proving that food has a large impact on our overall health and may even determine which diseases and ailments we will get later in life. The more we are aware of the importance of our food choices, the earlier we can teach and protect our children. Of course, there is always a balance to strike between what's good for our body and what's good for our taste buds and lifestyle. Here is a description of the most important nutrients for your child's development and which foods meet their needs.

IRON

Babies are born with their own source of iron, but this will be depleted after six months. Iron is absorbed best if it is from meat, such as beef, turkey, or chicken. However there are also iron-rich vegetarian foods, including dried apricots, molasses, fortified cereals, refined lentils, soybeans, and leafy green vegetables. The vegetarian baby can increase iron absorption by eating foods rich in vitamin C (citrus fruits, berries, tomatoes) with meals. Giving milk separately from meals also promotes iron absorption.

CALCIUM

Breast milk or formula provides all your baby's calcium needs initially. Calcium helps teeth and bones and promotes overall strength. Good sources later include cow's milk, fortified soy milk and orange juice, cheeses, molasses, dark green vegetables, dried beans, lentils, and tofu.

PROTEIN

Babies require more protein per pound of body weight than adults because of their rapid growth. A one-year-old child needs about fifteen grams of protein or two cups of high-protein food per day, such as milk, cheese, beans, tofu, fish, poultry, and lean meats. Combination foods such as grains (bread, pasta, rice) with beans, lentils, cheeses, or tofu will provide the balance needed for vegetarian babies.

VITAMIN B12

Vitamin B12 is usually found in animal products, such as meat and chicken. Non-meat sources include dairy products and eggs, as well as fortified foods such as soy milk and cereals.

VITAMIN D

Vitamin D is made as the result of sunlight on the skin. Most children in warm climates receive adequate Vitamin D if they spend twenty to thirty minutes a day, two to three times per week in the sun. Dietary sources of vitamin D include dairy products, eggs, and fortified foods. Breast milk or formula will provide vitamin D in the beginning stages. Some pediatricians recommend vitamin D supplements.

FIBER

Most of your baby's fiber needs will be met with fruits, vegetables, and cereal. Be careful as a diet too high in fiber and whole grains can fill up a child before his nutritional needs have been met and interfere with absorption of minerals such as zinc, iron, and calcium. Too much fiber may also cause your baby to have diarrhea or an upset stomach.

ZINC

Zinc is important for healthy immune systems and growth. Offer your child plenty of food rich in zinc such as wheat germ, lean meats, milk, lentils, dried beans, peas, corn, and soybeans. Zinc, like iron, may be a problem for vegetarian babies because of poor absorption.

FAT

Infants receive 40 to 50 percent of their calories from fat, through breast milk or formula. After the first twelve months, your baby will receive fat from whole cow's milk or soy milk. After age two, the Pediatric Panel of the National Cholesterol Education Program recommends reducing fat calories to 30 percent or less of the total calories. This is the time to switch from whole-fat milk products to low-fat versions. Healthy fat sources include walnuts, canola oil, avocados, milk, cheese, and yogurt.

ANTIOXIDANTS

These are important early on as they prevent damage to developing DNA. The average American family eats only 50 percent of what is recommended. Vegetables and fruits are the best source of antioxidants, including sweet potatoes, carrots, kiwi fruit, broccoli, avocados, and blueberries.

WATER

According to Melvin B. Heyman, M.D. and author of *Feeding Your Child For Lifelong Health*, 50 to 70 percent of a child's body is water. Babies get all of their required water early on from breast milk or formula. However, once solids are introduced babies need more liquids to aid swallowing and digestion and maintain hydration as they become more and more active. Offer water to your child both at mealtimes with food and alone throughout the day.

The nutrients listed above are good for all ages. While they contribute to your child's development they also keep adults healthy and free from diseases. You are the expert when it comes to your family and child. If you have a concern, trust your instincts and find someone to help you with health and nutrition questions and problems; pediatricians, nutritionists, dietitians, and lactation consultants are the perfect resources. Typically steady growth is the best proof that your child is getting the right amount of food.

Food Allergies and Intolerances

About 9 percent of babies have food allergies, while many others have food intolerances. Food allergies and intolerances can cause a wide range of respiratory and digestive symptoms, such as colic, vomiting, diarrhea, stomach discomfort, asthma, hives, and eczema. Food reactions are often difficult to diagnose as symptoms can come on quickly within minutes or hours or gradually over days or weeks.

Many people think allergies and intolerances are the same, but they involve different mechanisms in the body. While they may share similar symptoms, including diarrhea and vomiting, food allergy is an immune system response, usually to proteins. Food allergies start in the first year of life in about 80 percent of cases. Children, who have immature immune systems compared with adults, are most susceptible to a broad array of food allergies, which makes it logical to avoid certain highly potential allergic foods. Usually food allergies that develop early in infancy are outgrown by age three. However, people allergic to peanuts, tree nuts, and shellfish tend to have lifelong food triggers, and reactions to these foods may become more serious over time.

In food intolerances, small amounts of the problem food may be tolerated, unlike food allergies where even the smallest amount can trigger a reaction. Unfortunately, the body usually does not outgrow a food intolerance.

The best way to avoid allergies and intolerances is by introducing the most common offending foods cautiously and at the appropriate age and stage. If you suspect your child has a food intolerance or allergy, consult your pediatrician about symptoms and concerns and try to identify the offensive food in order to eliminate it from your child's diet. Here are a few tips when feeding children with adverse food reactions.

- ◆ Check ingredient labels of processed foods that may contain traces of the food.

- ◆ When dining in restaurants or friends' homes, ask about menu ingredients and preparation to avoid potential risks to your child.

- Tell your family and the child's caregivers about foods to avoid when your child is in their care.

- When available, use alternative ingredients in recipes and favorite foods so your child does not feel excluded or different, such as substituting soy or rice "milk" in recipes that call for cow's milk.

Special Diets as a Lifestyle Choice

Parents control their children's diets from their first bite. And some parents wish to raise their children on a vegetarian or vegan diet with the rest of the family. Whether the reason is health or politically motivated, you can find foods that will satisfy your child's palate and still sustain their body.

RAISING VEGETARIAN BABIES

In the beginning, providing your baby with a vegetarian diet is not that different from the diet of a baby who eats meat. Babies on either diet receive breast milk or formula and eat cereals, fruits, and vegetables at the appropriate time. However, instead of being introduced to meat (during the Independent stage, see page 100) the vegetarian baby will be offered mashed tofu or dried beans as a source of nutrients and protein. The important thing for any baby's diet is balanced foods and combinations of proteins, fruits, and vegetables.

Nutritional requirements for all babies are high, as they need protein, calcium, and other nutrients for healthy brain and body development. However, it is possible for a vegetarian diet to provide for all your baby's needs. For babies with a more narrow diet it is particularly important to introduce foods and textures repeatedly. Your baby's palate may reject stronger-tasting vegetables such as broccoli, cauliflower, and cabbage, during the first months of solid foods, but he may like them months later. So if you're set on feeding a vegetarian diet, don't give up too soon.

RAISING VEGAN BABIES

Veganism is a vegetarian diet, devoid of all dairy products and animal by-products. This diet for children has raised controversy because of the latest version of Dr.

Benjamin Spock's *Baby and Child Care* book. The updated nutritional advice in this bestseller, first published fifty-two years ago, advises parents that it is okay to follow a vegan diet for children after they are two years old.

Most nutritionists, including Ellyn Sater, author of *Child of Mine: Feeding with Love and Good Sense*, disagree and are concerned that children could get into trouble nutritionally, as the more foods you cut out of your child's diet, the greater the risk for nutritional deficiencies. One major challenge of the vegan diet is the lack of iron absorbed by the body. Jill Stovsky, Baby Center's in-house nutritional expert cautions parents, "I would recommend a vegan diet only if somebody really knows how to do it—has the knowledge, the background, the time and the vigilance to do it."

Parents who want to raise their baby on a vegan or vegetarian diet should consult their physician to be sure all the child's nutritional needs can be met. Your pediatrician may prescribe a dietary supplement to babies and children who may not be getting enough iron and other nutrients in their diets.

Special Diets Due to Illness and Other Restrictions

For parents of children with dietary restrictions, learning to cook healthy meals to meet their needs can be a challenge. Beside each recipe in this book there are icons to illustrate some of the common dietary restrictions, so it is easy to identify which foods will meet your family's health needs and dietary lifestyle choices. Here are some of the most common children's health issues that can be managed and affected by diet.

CELIAC

Celiac or celiac sprue is a potentially devastating digestive disorder that's triggered by gluten, a protein found in wheat, barley, and rye. The body views this protein as an enemy and creates antibodies in response. Untreated, the disease can result in malnutrition, anemia, diabetes, osteoporosis, and a range of other diseases.

According to Dr. Peter Green, gastroenterologist and head of the Celiac Disease Center at Columbia University, celiac may be the most misdiagnosed illness around. A recent study suggests the disease affects one in 133 Americans, but is only diagnosed in about one in four thousand. Symptoms include failure to thrive in infants, developmental delays, slow weight gain, chronic diarrhea, anemia, muscle cramps, bone loss, and joint pain.

The disease is managed with a gluten- and wheat-free diet. Parents of children with celiac disease must keep a watchful eye out for unsuspecting products that contain gluten. Read labels very carefully as "grains are used as filler in soups and several other canned goods, as well as in medications, soy sauce, some toothpastes, and even in the glue you lick on an envelope," says the mother of two-and-a-half-year-old Eamon's and nine-year-old Colin, who have the disease. Some celiacs can tolerate oats while others cannot. Other ingredients to watch out for include: rye, spelt, barley, and distilled vinegar. Use alternative flours such as white rice, brown rice, soy, and arrowroot. For resources of where to buy gluten-free products, see page 255. You'll also find recipes throughout the book that are gluten-free.

DIABETES

Diabetes is a chronic, debilitating disease affecting every organ system of the body. There are two major types of the disease. Type I, or insulin-dependent diabetes, is also called "juvenile diabetes," because it usually strikes in childhood. For some reason the insulin-producing cells of the pancreas fail to produce insulin, and thus the person must inject insulin on a daily basis. According to the Juvenile Diabetes Research Foundation, diabetes is one of the most costly, chronic diseases of childhood and one that is never outgrown. Type II diabetes, or noninsulin dependent diabetes, is sometimes called "adult-onset diabetes" as it is usually diagnosed in adulthood and does not require the use of insulin. However the increased rate of childhood obesity has led to an epidemic in cases of type II diabetes in young adults and children under ten years old.

According to diabetes researchers, the only effective way to prevent and control Type II diabetes in children is to promote a more healthful pattern of growth and development. Because children are growing so rapidly, they need plenty of calories and nutrients from a diet rich in fruits, vegetables, beans, whole grains, nuts, lean protein foods, and nonfat dairy products. In addition, as the child grows, a minimum of one hour of physical activity each day is crucial for both physical development and weight management.

OBESITY

Obesity is a condition characterized by excessive body fat. In 2002 at the largest conference ever held on childhood obesity, the U.S. Surgeon General Dr. Richard Carmona said that obesity is the fastest growing cause of illness and death in the United States and said it deserved more attention than any other epidemic. According to doctors, obesity is pulling the trigger on many illnesses, including the four-fold increase of type II diabetes over the last ten years. Many experts blame childhood obesity and health risks on a lack of exercise and trend to "supersize" portions of food and sugary drinks. A nutritionist or pediatrician can help with portion control and exercise programs. Parents can help by ridding the cupboards of processed and high-fat foods, sugary snacks, and sodas, and stocking up on whole foods and healthy alternatives.

ANEMIA

This is a condition in which the blood is deficient in red blood cells, in hemoglobin, or in total volume. Nine percent of children younger than three have iron-deficiency anemia (IDA) and even more are iron deficient without being anemic. According to nutritionist Maria Pari-Keener, not getting an adequate amount of iron is the most common nutritional deficiency. The symptoms of anemia include a lack of vitality, pale complexion, and colorless lips and eyelids. Anemia puts babies at risk for delayed mental and motor skills development, learning difficulties, and even heart trouble.

IDA is very treatable with dietary changes and if necessary, supplementary iron drops. Most babies get plenty of iron their first six months through iron-fortified formula or breast milk. However, after six months babies require more iron than can be absorbed from formula and breast milk. Thus babies who are not offered solids or who refuse them have the potential to become anemic early on because they are not getting iron from cereals, fruits, and vegetables. Toddlerhood is another risk period, because children are no longer consuming iron-fortified formula and are now drinking cow's milk, which interferes with the absorption of iron. In addition, they may be filling up on juices and other beverages and not getting a variety of whole foods that contain iron and essential nutrients.

The RDA (recommended daily allowance) of iron is at least eleven milligrams for babies seven to twelve months old, and at least seven milligrams for toddlers ages one to three years old.

Iron-Rich Foods for Your Baby and Toddler

FOR BABIES	FOR TODDLERS
Dry infant cereal, 1 tablespoon: 1.1 mg	Blackstrap molasses (adds moisture/sweetness to baked goods), 1 tablespoon: 7.5 mg
Iron-fortified formula, 8 ounces: 1.8 mg	
Egg yolk, one: .6 mg	Beef (hamburgers, roast beef sandwiches, fajitas), 1 ounce: 1.5 mg
Toasted oat cereal, 2 tablespoons: 1 mg	
	Soybeans (dried or edamame), 1/2 cup cooked dried: 2.5 mg
	Avocado (mashed, cut into salads, or spread on sandwiches and tortillas), 1 medium: 2.0 mg
	Dried apricots (add to granola, cereal, yogurt), 1/4 cup: 2 mg
	Fresh peas (cooked, add to couscous, pasta, rice), 1/2 cup: 1.5 mg

LACTOSE INTOLERANCE

The most common intolerance is to lactose or milk sugar, the carbohydrate in milk. Those who are lactose intolerant do not have the ability to digest lactose in milk, because they do not produce enough of the enzyme lactase (lactase deficiency). Lactase is needed to break lactose down into simpler sugars so the body can absorb them. Symptoms include stomachache, diarrhea, and bloating. Usually the intolerance is not complete and small amounts of milk can be consumed. Seventy percent of adults are considered to be lactose intolerant. Symptoms include stomachache, diarrhea, and gas.

MILK ALLERGY

Lactose intolerance is uncommon in children under age three, but many children have an allergy to milk protein. This milk aversion is a negative reaction to lactoglobulin, a crystalline protein faction from the whey of milk. If your child cannot process milk proteins your doctor will probably suggest soy- or rice-based formula, milk, cheese, and yogurt. Be sure to check ingredient labels for "casein" and "whey," as these also indicate the presence of milk proteins.

COLIC

Colic is characterized by long bouts of inconsolable crying for three or more hours, three or more times per week. While there is no consensus about what causes colic or how to stop it, some doctors believe that a child's diet can enhance or diminish the symptoms of colic. These doctors believe a baby's immature digestive system causes gas and pain, and thus a baby's diet, as well as the nursing mother's, can contribute to this problem.

GAS-PRODUCING FOODS

Foods that are thought to cause gas and colic include dairy, milk, dark green vegetables, onions, dried beans, and spicy foods. If you believe a food is to blame for your child's discomfort, try avoiding it for a few days.

GERD OR REFLUX

Many babies will spit up after eating, because their digestive system is immature and the esophageal sphincter, the muscle that holds the stomach contents in place, doesn't close tight enough. However some babies have Gastro Esophageal Reflux Disease (GERD), which causes frequent and painful vomiting after each meal and little or no weight gain. Most children will grow out of this when their system is fully developed; however, you should speak to your pediatrician for diagnosis and treatment. Reflux can be treated with medication to ease the pain and promote weight gain. However the problem could be pyloric stenosis, a narrowing of the outlet between the stomach and small intestine, which prevents the stomach from emptying. This usually occurs in babies six months or younger and must be corrected with surgery.

Chapter 4

Parenting in the Kitchen

Please pass the love, unity, and spaghetti. An unlikely request? Perhaps. But in truth, that's what you give your child when you sit down together at the family table.

CONNIE EVERS, R.D.

KITCHENS ARE THE HUB OF THE HOME and where everything happens. It's not just where you prepare and eat your food. Cooking and eating with friends and family creates an atmosphere to connect, share, and interact, to nourish the body, the soul, and the spirit. For parents the kitchen makes a great classroom to teach—and learn—a variety of lessons. The key is to get children involved.

Establishing Routine

Creating routine and ritual is important for instilling good eating habits. In the beginning you and your baby will have a routine for just about all aspects of life. Keeping a schedule sets expectations for both parents and children, and allows you to anticipate your child's needs and be prepared to meet them. Children need a consistent eating and snack schedule and a variety of healthy foods. This helps them regulate their appetites and expand their tastes. The predictability of mealtimes is emotionally reassuring for young eaters.

Sara Duskin, lactation consultant, recommends feeding your child in a highchair from the very beginning. When they are first eating solids, you will need to be sure they are properly supported, as they will not be able to sit up by themselves. Sitting in the chair is an early signal to them that it is time to eat. The chair will provide more safety for them and more convenience for you. Your hands will be free for spooning, and you can now face each other to watch and interact. Over time, sitting still may become more difficult for your active toddler. They may want to eat on the go or while playing. This should be avoided as it increases the possibility of choking and decreases the social interaction and nurturing that mealtimes provide. Establishing a seat at the table early on will help social and concentration skills later.

Try to choose one meal each day where every family member comes to the table. Most parents think the family meal must be dinner, and must be a "hot meal." This is not the case. Establish a routine that works for you. Whether it's eating breakfast foods for dinner or sharing a picnic at lunch, allow enough time to enjoy the meal and the company without rushing. As your child gets older this may become more of a challenge, but starting early promotes the importance of family time together.

Socializing in the Kitchen

Children like to be with their parents and where the action is happening. Here are some ideas for socializing with your children while in the kitchen.

- Provide a drawer in the kitchen that they can open and pick out cooking tools to play with. Children love playing with simple pots, pans, and wooden spoons. My son, Jonas's, favorite kitchen toy is a whisk.

- Find a place that's safe for them to watch you cook, but also allows you to engage with them. "When my son was first born, he sat in his bouncy seat on the floor. Later I would move his highchair into the kitchen, for a safe bird's-eye view," says eleven-month-old Jack's mom.

- When eating, sit at the table. Take the time to sit and relax over a meal. Even though your meal may be quick to make, take the time to eat and enjoy it.

- Talk with children at mealtimes. Show them respect and include them in the dinner conversation.

- Create a stress-free feeding and eating environment. Let your child concentrate on eating without phone or television interruptions and distractions.

Early Learning

Besides cooking, you can teach many skills and lessons while in the kitchen.

- ◆ "Explore all the senses," says Gayle Pirie, chef/owner of Foreign Cinema Restaurant. Use fingers to touch and play with food, smell the aroma, see the presentation of a dish, hear the sounds of food cooking, and, of course, taste the food.

- ◆ Colors and numbers. Have your child count the numbers of apples you're peeling and ask the color of the apples.

- ◆ Vocabulary. Recite the names of all your ingredients and ask your child to repeat the words, and even try to spell them.

- ◆ Safety. Show children the potential dangers in the kitchen, what not to touch and why.

- ◆ Agriculture and gardening. Tell children how their fruits and vegetables grow and where their food comes from. Consider planting a garden or a window box, so they will witness the growing process. "We grow our own produce, so we have really good food. Plus, our children get involved by picking the fruits and vegetables," says Rebecca Marder, chef and owner of Capo Restaurant in Los Angeles and mother of four.

- ◆ Table manners and etiquette. Teach the use of utensils, and practice saying please and thank you.

- ◆ Following directions. A recipe can help with reading comprehension and how to complete individual tasks.

Cooking with a Baby

Many people say they can't cook, because they have no time and the baby won't let them. Making healthy meals for your family does not require a specific recipe or continuous hours of time alone in the kitchen. You only need an imagination, a stocked pantry (see page 13 for tips on Stocking a Kitchen) and these ideas for making meals despite interruptions.

- Find a safe place for baby to watch you cook.

- Talk to your baby if they can't see you cooking, to comfort and remind them you are near.

- Remember to take breaks when cooking to spend a few minutes playing or hugging.

- Play music your child enjoys, sing, and do a few dance moves while cooking. (I know this sounds silly, but it's supposed to be. My son laughs at me in the kitchen all the time.)

- Interruptions will happen. Make foods that can be prepped easily, by taking advantage of short-cut ingredients.

- Take advantage of times when your child is sleeping and napping to prep foods without interruption.

- Make large portions so you can freeze meals and thaw at your convenience.

- Prepare one-dish meals such as soups, chili, and lasagna that can cook unattended for long periods.

Cooking with a Toddler

Teach children how to make family recipes and tell them stories about your childhood and mealtimes with their grandparents. Contributing to the family meal can provide a boost in self-esteem. They will take pride and be emotionally invested in what they've chosen. They will eat the meal and encourage others to do so. You'll be surprised what they've learned by watching you cook and want to show you what they can do. Here are some ways to get them involved:

- Take children shopping and allow them to choose foods for the family.

- Let them help with kitchen tasks such as kneading dough, sorting vegetables, decorating cookies, or making place cards.

- Be flexible and allow your child to be creative with recipe ideas and ingredients.

- Give them a show. Pretend you're on a cooking show and explain to your child what you're doing to keep them interested. When they're ready they can act out a culinary show for you.

- Take time to cook with them, but remember tasks will take longer.

- Children will spill and make mistakes when cooking. Be patient!

> *Growing up, I was the Official Taste Tester. When my mother was cooking, she would give me a bite of an ingredient to make sure it was "good" and could be added to the dish. I took this job seriously and felt like I'd contributed something special to the meal.*
>
> LISA, thirty-five-year-old

Developing Positive Attitudes

Children will pick up on your attitude toward food and notice what and how you eat. If you are always dieting and not enjoying food, you may pass along negative feelings about food to your children.

- Have them see you enjoying wholesome foods.

- Avoid eating foods in front of children that you don't want them to eat. If they see you eating cookies, they will want cookies, too.

- Speak positively and encourage discussion about foods and nutrition.

- Avoid forcing them to eat. They can manage their own appetite and will eat when and if they are hungry.

- Introduce a variety of flavors, textures, and colors to your children's diet.

- Eat whole foods vs. "fast" foods.

- Avoid bribing children with sweets and desserts. Give everything in moderation, so the treat isn't forbidden and thus becomes too special.

Combating Outside Influences

In your own home you have control over your child's diet including what and how much they eat. However, there are many outside influences such as day care, schools, friends, family, and even television to challenge your child's taste buds and health. It is up to you to teach your children the basic information about whole foods and introduce them to a wide variety of tastes in hopes they will make healthy choices outside your table. As a parent you can also discuss healthy eating habits and give instructions to teachers, family members, and caregivers about the foods you'd like them to both encourage and avoid when your child is in their care.

The most important thing you can do to instill good eating habits, according to pediatrician Brock Bernstein, M.D., is to offer healthy food choices whenever possible. "Children will go through phases, but just keep offering a healthy, balanced, organic, and pesticide-free diet."

Parents definitely need to do a better job of regulating the junk, but outside pressure is everywhere! There's a constant barrage in schools and supermarkets. And don't even get me started on the nutritional deficiencies of restaurant "kid" menus and of "healthy snacks" that are just glorified candy.

Letter to *Parents* magazine from a concerned mom in Ohio

Serving a Variety of Foods, Flavors, and Textures

Research shows that lifelong food preferences are formed in the first few years. University of Tennessee researchers surveyed over one hundred children ages two to eight about their food likes and dislikes. They found that 70% of food preferences were established by age two.

—*American Baby* magazine, September 2004

It's easy to make the same foods over and over; however, your child's palate will be limited. The wider the variety of tastes and textures you introduce to your baby early on, the more foods they'll eat and enjoy as children and later adults. This also means if they are offered healthy foods from a young age, they will choose those same foods as they age. By offering a rainbow of colors of fruits and vegetables you'll also ensure your child is eating a wide range of vitamins and minerals. Take advantage of the time when your baby "puts everything in his mouth." This is a window of opportunity to offer new tastes, foods, and experiences. Remember that eating involves all the senses. It's more than just how a particular food tastes to your child. How does it feel in your baby's mouth, and squished in her hands? What does she smell when you're cooking her food? What does she see when she looks at her breakfast? What are the sounds your child hears as she chews? These are all new experiences for your little one.

> *"I didn't know what to make anymore. Jake seemed bored with the same purees and soft foods. But I wasn't sure what to give next. His grandma let him bite into a raw apple and he thought that was the greatest. Now he'll try anything that crunches."*
>
> —SIXTEEN-MONTH-OLD JAKE'S mom

New or different foods don't have to be elaborate recipes or vegetables you've never seen and can't pronounce. Think of new ways to cook, cut, and present your family's favorite foods. You may only think of sweet potatoes as a Thanksgiving treat, when you get out your family recipe for baked sweet potatoes with marshmallows. But think about all the other great ways you can enjoy sweet potatoes—pureed, baked in the oven, stuffed with chili or vegetables, cut and baked as chips and served with dip, or even transformed into a hearty soup. If you sell your child short and assume she won't eat it, you'll never know, and miss an opportunity. Your child won't always want or like something new, but that's okay. The only thing you can do is offer.

> *"We were out for sushi and she wanted to try my California roll, so I let her. I thought she'd spit it out, but she didn't, and wanted more. I can't believe I have a three-year-old who likes sushi."*
>
> —THREE-YEAR-OLD LEYLA'S mom

Creating Comfort

What keeps me motivated is not the food itself but all the bonds and memories the food represents.

MICHAEL CHIARELLO, cookbook author and chef

Food can remind us of childhood, special occasions, events, people, and places. Usually these "comfort foods" are rich in flavor and texture, and may reflect an ethnic heritage, culture, or region. We rely on these foods to comfort us when we're not feeling well, or when we want to be reminded of a special time, event, or feeling. Comfort foods are personal tastes and different for everyone.

The flavor and food item is not the focus; it's the emotion and memories that are brought up when preparing and eating them. They may be time consuming to make, such as a Thanksgiving dinner, or they may be as quick and easy as a peanut butter and banana sandwich. Think about what foods and recipes you and your children bond over, and which ones will become your child's comfort foods and why.

James loves to "help" in the kitchen and watch me cook. One day we were at the park and James fell while running and scraped his knee. He was bleeding and crying as I ran over to him. While I was checking his knee, he sobbed, "I want to make spaghetti."

THREE-YEAR-OLD JAMES'S mother

Have Fun

Often this is the part parents learn from their children. If you think of cooking and meals as a chore, so will your children. However if you take a cue from your kids and get messy, create silly menus, and play with food, it will be an adventure. Of course you can't make every meal a holiday, full of games and surprises, but here are a few ways to get creative and keep you and your family interested in food and meals.

- ◆ Arrange food in funny faces and animals, such as a smiley face of raisins in the oatmeal.

- Create fun shapes in ordinary foods. How about heart-shaped tortillas or four-leaf clover sandwiches?

- Personalize the meal. Use a squeeze bottle to write your child's name in cheese sauce over their vegetables.

- Have theme nights around a menu. Don't forget decorations and costumes.

> *When I make pancakes, I put the batter in a squeeze bottle and draw pictures on the griddle. My son is really into hockey now, so I've been using the team logos for inspiration.*
>
> THREE-AND-A-HALF-YEAR-OLD BROOK'S mom
>
> *One sure way to get my son to eat is to have "shish kabob night." He'll eat stuff on a toothpick that he won't eat cut up on the plate. I put ham, cheese, pickles, carrots, broccoli . . . whatever looks good on a toothpick. Sometimes he wants me to put the food on the toothpick and sometimes he likes to create his own.*
>
> FOUR-YEAR-OLD BRIAN'S mom

Chapter 5

Food Safety Lessons

W E DON'T USUALLY WORRY ABOUT our food being safe or making us ill, until we see a story on the news related to mad cow disease or E. coli. However, there are less severe cases of germs and bacteria that are found in foods every day. You may not feel well, not because you have a cold or flu, but because you've eaten food that was handled or prepared in an unsafe manner. There are many things you can do in your kitchen to be sure the food you are preparing for your family is not only of high quality, but also free from harmful bacteria and contaminates. Adapted from the National Registry of Food Safety Professionals, here are ten simple food safety tips, that together spell:

F-o-o-d S-a-f-e-t-y

Fight bacteria by washing your hands often. Wash for about twenty seconds (sing "Row, Row, Row Your Boat" twice) with hot, soapy water BEFORE fixing or eating foods and AFTER using the bathroom, changing diapers, handling pets, gardening, coughing, or blowing your nose.

According to a Penn State University study of mothers with infants less than four months old:

- 32 percent said they don't wash their hands after changing their baby's diaper;

- about 15 percent said they don't wash their hands after using the bathroom;

- about 10 percent don't wash their hands after handling raw meat;

- about 41 percent don't wash their hands after petting animals.

Not washing hands could result in infant diarrhea from the bacteria picked up by hands in the activities cited. (Source: What You Need to Know About Food Safety & Young Children, FDA/Center for Food Safety, 5/99)

Only thaw perishable food in the refrigerator or the microwave. Never defrost food on the kitchen counter. Cook food immediately after thawing in a microwave.

Order perishable hot takeout foods so they're delivered shortly before serving. Whether takeout or prepared at home, hold hot food above 140°F and cold foods below 40°F. Avoid letting foods sit at room temperature longer than two hours.

Divide leftovers into small, shallow containers for rapid cooling in the refrigerator.

Set your refrigerator to run at 40°F and your freezer at 0°F to help stop harmful bacteria from growing. Keep an appliance thermometer in your refrigerator/freezer to monitor temperatures.

Avoid cross-contamination. Wash cutting boards, knives, and other utensils in the dishwasher or with hot soapy water and rinse with hot water after they come in contact with raw meat, poultry, and seafood, and before using them for another item. Avoid placing cooked food on a plate that held these raw foods. Several colored plastic cutting boards can help keep food types separate, to avoid cross-contamination. Wooden cutting boards should be wiped with a solution of bleach and water.

Fruits and vegetables should be thoroughly cleaned before eating. According to the Center for Science in the Public Interest in Washington, D.C., 28 percent of all food poisoning cases are caused by contaminated produce. Wash fruits and vegetables thoroughly (for about thirty seconds) with running tap water just before eating. Firm vegetables such as apples and potatoes should also be scrubbed with a vegetable brush. There are citrus-based fruit and vegetable washes that can be purchased at health and grocery stores. Clean skin and peels even if you don't plan to eat it. That way, bacteria on such items as melons and cucumbers won't be passed from the outside to the inside when the food is cut. Do not assume "ready to eat" packaged produce has already been washed.

Eat foods that you know are safe. Most of the bacteria that commonly cause food-borne illness can't be seen, smelled, or tasted. When in doubt, toss it out!

Take the cooked temperature of perishable foods such as meat, poultry, and seafood to assure harmful bacteria are destroyed. Cook hamburger and other ground meats (veal, lamb, and pork) to an internal temperature of 160°F and ground poultry to 165°F. Beef, veal, and lamb steaks and roasts may be cooked to 145°F for medium rare and to 160°F for medium. Whole poultry should be cooked to 180°F as measured in the thigh; breast meat to 170°F. All cuts of pork should reach 160°F. Thoroughly cook fish until it is opaque and flakes with a fork.

Yolks and whites of eggs should be cooked until firm to avoid possible food-borne illness from salmonella. Store fresh eggs in their original carton, and use within three weeks for the best quality. Use hard-cooked eggs within one week, and do not return them to the egg carton for storage. Refrigerate them in a clean container.

Due to food quality and special preparation methods in restaurants and homes, some of these rules may not be adhered. Your favorite Caesar salad dressing may contain raw egg yolks, and a restaurant chef may recommend your pork chop be cooked to only 145°F. Usually your food server or menu will warn you about such items, so you can make an informed decision regarding your food choices. These items will probably not hurt you; however, babies and young children are more susceptible to illness, thus your choices for them should be more cautious. If you are concerned about a certain food or food preparation method, avoid those items.

Babies usually triple their birth weight the first year of life. That's why nutritious and safely handled food, served in an age-appropriate way, is so important. In addition to the general food safety rules above, there are some specific tips (see below) for feeding infants. A recent study in the *Journal of Nutrition Education* showed that over time mothers received conflicting and sometimes inaccurate information, particularly from relatives and friends about feeding their children ages two months to four years.

Many advise about how much, what and when to feed an infant child, but the following feeding practices may not be mentioned. While some of these tips may seem basic, they are important to remember and teach to your child's caregivers.

1. Handle Bottles Carefully. Although some babies will drink a bottle straight from the refrigerator, the American Academy of Pediatrics (AAP) advises most babies prefer milk warmed to room temperature. Warm the bottle by holding it under a running hot-water faucet or putting it in a bowl of hot water for a few minutes. Shake well and test the milk temperature to make sure it's not too hot before feeding. Microwaves can heat unevenly.

The Centers for Disease Control and Prevention warn that children's mouths and throats can be severely burned by bottles heated in the microwave. Always discard leftover milk from a bottle to reduce harmful bacteria.

2. Feed Solids Safely. Never leave a baby alone with any food and not properly strapped in a feeding chair.

3. Avoid Honey and Corn Syrup. Do not serve infants honey or corn syrup during the first year of life. These foods may contain botulism spores that could cause illness or death in infants. They do not cause problems for older children and adults.

4. Avoid Harmful Bacteria. Transfer an amount you feel baby will eat from the baby food jar or storage container to another dish. Throw away any food left uneaten in the dish. Bacteria from a baby's mouth can grow and multiply in the food before it is served again. Too many bacteria can make a baby sick. Use baby food within one to two days after opening.

5. Heat Food Cautiously. Serve foods warm, but not hot. If using a microwave oven be aware that they can produce "hot spots" in food that can scald a baby's mouth. Food in a baby food jar can also spit and boil over in your microwave. No matter how you are heating foods for baby, be sure to test the temperature on your lips or with a special temperature spoon that changes color if food is too hot.

6. Practice the Two-Hour Rule. Never leave foods, raw or cooked, at room temperature longer than two hours (if a hot day over 90°F, no longer than one hour). This includes jarred baby food, once opened. Bacteria can grow to harmful levels when food is left out longer than this.

7. Pack Food Safely. If packing a bottle or lunch for travel or school, use an ice source to keep perishable foods cold (below 40°F). Some foods such as yogurt can be frozen and added to lunches to keep other foods cool. A soft-sided insulated bag (with a freezer block) is a convenient method for packing foods. Hot foods should be kept hot (above 140°F) when traveling, by using a thermos or other insulated container.

Food Storage

When showing parents how to pack foods for their refrigerator and freezer they often ask, "How long will that last?" Following is a chart of common foods and their shelf, refrigerator, or freezer life adapted from the Food Marketing Institute (FMI). Of course this is only a guide. If you are suspicious of a food item because of packaging changes, smell, color, or taste—throw it away.

WHAT ABOUT PACKAGE DATES?

Most product dating is not required by federal regulations, but dating of some foods is required by more than half the states. Infant formula and baby foods are required by law to have a "use by" date. Calendar dates are found primarily on perishable foods such as dairy, eggs, meats, and poultry. Coded dates may appear on shelf-stable products packaged in boxes and cans. Here is a definition of dates:

◆ "Sell By" tells the store how long to display the product for sale. Buy the product before this date.

FOOD ITEM	REFRIGERATOR/COOL PANTRY	FREEZER
Eggs, fresh in shell	3 weeks	12 months, beaten (do not freeze in shell)
Milk, opened	5 to 7 days	4 weeks
Yogurt, opened	7 to 10 days	6 weeks
Butter	7 to 14 days	6 to 9 months
Cottage cheese, opened	7 to 14 days	
Hard or wax-coated cheeses (cheddar, Swiss, Gouda)	3 to 6 months, unopened 3 to 4 weeks, opened 2 weeks, sliced or grated	1 to 2 months
Lunch meat	2 weeks, unopened 3 to 5 days, opened	1 to 2 months
Raw ground meats (hamburger, turkey, lamb, pork, veal)	1 to 2 days	1 to 2 months
Fresh meats (steaks, chops, roasts)	3 to 5 days	6 to 12 months
Fresh poultry	1 to 2 days	9 to 12 months
Leftovers, cooked meats, and meat dishes	3 to 4 days	2 to 3 months
Leftovers, cooked poultry dishes	3 to 4 days	4 to 6 months
Fresh fish	1 day	2 to 3 months
Flours	3 to 4 months	8 months
Grains and pastas	3 to 6 months	
Fresh produce	4 to 7 days	3 to 4 months (cooked)

◆ "Best If Used By" recommended for best flavor and quality. Not a safety date.

◆ "Use By" the last date recommended by manufacturer to use product while at its peak quality.

◆ "Closed or Coded" packing numbers for use by the manufacturer in tracking their product. Will be able to locate if a recall.

Knowing safe food handling practices, being aware of potential food dangers to your child, and storing food properly are the best ways to protect your family from food illnesses and accidents while also giving your child a healthy start on development and growth.

Chapter 6

Organics and Other Food Buzzwords

Understanding Organic

Organic products were produced in response to consumer concerns in the 1970s regarding safe food and water, pesticides in food, the environment, pollution, and overall food quality. Organic means grown or raised without toxic pesticides, herbicides, fungicides, synthetic fertilizer, hormones, antibiotics, genetically modified ingredients, or irradiation. Thus, no artificial or chemical measures can be used during the growing process.

Prior to October 2002, there were no governing standards for using the term *organic* on food labels in the U.S. According to Barbara Robinson, USDA deputy administrator in charge of the National Organic Program, "every state and every organization had its own standard for what was organic. So the meaning depended on who was using it at the time." As of October 21, 2002, the USDA created uniform national standards for any American grower or food processor labeling their food organic. Only those products that are all or at least 95 percent organic can be certified by a government approved agency and use the official USDA organic label. The requirements for being certified as an organic food producer prohibit the use of all of the following materials and practices:

TOXIC SYNTHETIC PESTICIDES AND FERTILIZERS

A farm must be free from these chemicals for at least three years before a certified crop can be grown.

SEWAGE SLUDGE

Although widely used by nonorganic farms, sewage sludge is prohibited in the production of organic foods because of toxic chemicals and heavy metals, called "biosolids," which can cause soil contamination.

FRESH MANURE

Proper animal care and manure composting techniques are mandatory and require a waiting period between the application of raw manure and the harvest of any organic crops that are likely to be eaten raw.

IRRADIATION

The controversial technology of exposing food to radiation to kill microorganisms and preserve food items is banned in certified organic foods.

ORGANIC EVERYTHING

The list of organic offerings is staggering: carrots, hot dogs, chips, cheese, cake mix, hamburger, pasta, ice cream, soda, salsa, and more! The new labeling regulations

LABELS AND DEFINITIONS

100 percent organic: All ingredients are organic.

Organic: At least 95 percent of ingredients are organic.

Made with organic ingredients: At least 70 percent of ingredients are organic.

If less than 70 percent of the ingredients are organic, the word *organic* can be mentioned on the information panel, but not on the front of the package.

allow for various levels of organic, so it's up to you as the consumer to know what you are buying.

SINGLE INGREDIENTS

Single ingredients are those that are whole foods and not combined or processed with any other ingredients. Examples include carrots, apples, grapes, flour, and almonds. When you're shopping for single ingredients, look for the official USDA organic seal to know whether that product has met the government standard.

MULTIPLE INGREDIENTS

Multiple ingredients are those that are processed to combine single ingredients. These items include everything from bread to ketchup. If you're buying products with multiple ingredients, you need to understand the labeling hierarchy (see box page 45). Some ingredients in the product will be organic and others will not. To make the healthiest choice for your money on multiple-ingredient foods, do not stop at the organic claim. Remember to review the ingredient label as well.

ORGANICALLY RAISED ANIMALS

The USDA organic label also vouches for land-based animals such as pigs, cattle, lamb, and chicken. Growing consumer concerns regarding food safety, over use of antibiotics and mad-cow disease are driving the market toward more natural methods of raising meats and pork. Here are other terms that have become buzzwords when choosing meats and animal products such as milk and eggs.

- **Raised Organically** is the term for animals raised on 100 percent organic feed (grain or grass), without the use of synthetic hormones, antibiotics, or animal by-products. The animals have been allowed to roam outdoors and have access to pastures, rather than confined in small spaces and cages their entire life.

- **100% Grass-fed** or **100% Pasture-Finished** means the animals have spent their whole lives on pasture and never fed any grain products. The end result is a less fatty meat that contains higher levels of Omega-3s and conjugated linoleic acid, which have been linked to preventing cancer and diabetes.

- **The American Humane Association (AHA) Free Farmed label** certifies that animals are raised in a humane manner, with ample living space, adequate shelter, and comfortable resting areas.

- **Natural** is defined vaguely by the USDA as processed with no artificial ingredients. It can simply mean that the beef hasn't been altered with food coloring or artificial additives or that it was raised without the use of antibiotics, hormones, or animal proteins. Mel Coleman of Coleman Natural Meats in Denver believes this vague definition has led consumers to be desensitized to the claim.

- **No Antibiotics/No Hormones.** Many animals that live in crowded cages and pens are given antibiotics to prevent diseases, and hormones are commonly used commercially in animals such as dairy cows to increase milk production. Some hormones are natural, while others are synthetic, such as rBGH (bovine growth hormone) or genetically modified. If the product is labeled as no antibiotics or no hormones, the animals have not been treated.

ORGANICALLY RAISED FISH?

Seafood is a good source of high-quality protein and nutrients, especially fatty fish such as salmon, which contains essential omega oils. Unfortunately there are no organic or natural labels regarding fish, as the food and water contaminants cannot be completely eliminated for either wild or farm raised fish. However as of fall 2004, there is a seafood labeling law that requires seafood sold in U.S. supermarkets to carry labels stating where it was caught, where it was processed, and whether it was farmed or wild. To carry the U.S. country of origin label, farmed fish and shellfish must be derived exclusively from fish or shellfish hatched, raised, and processed in the U.S.

- **Farm Raised.** This term means fillets, steaks, nuggets, and any other flesh from a farm raised fish or shellfish.

- **Wild.** This refers to fish that are naturally born or hatchery raised, including shellfish harvested in the wild.

MERCURY IN FISH

The current advisory from the Food and Drug Administration regarding fish is regarding the possibility of high levels of methyl mercury in fish. Mercury occurs naturally in the environment. However the primary source in fish is from power plants that burn fossil fuels, especially coal. Through rain, snow, and runoff, mercury can accumulate in streams, oceans, rivers, and lakes, and aided by bacteria, it can undergo a transformation into methyl mercury, which can be toxic. Larger fish have accumulated the most methyl mercury, because they feed on other fish throughout their lives.

Methyl mercury can be harmful to the developing brains of unborn children and young children, as it can have an effect on their cognitive motor and sensory functions. The younger the person at the time of exposure and the greater the exposure to methyl mercury, the more significant the effects are likely to be. The key to healthfully enjoying a diet that includes fish is to eat a variety of different species, rather than focus on a single type in order to get the health benefits and reduce risks. The Environmental Protection Agency and National Academy of Sciences recommend limiting young children's fish consumption to one three-ounce meal of fish per week.

FISH WITH HIGHEST MERCURY LEVELS

The FDA advises pregnant woman and young children to avoid those fish that have the highest levels of mercury. These include: mackerel, shark, swordfish, tile fish, and fresh tuna.

The species of tuna used for canned tuna tends to be smaller than the longer living tuna in the fresh market. Choose "chunk light" or "chunk tuna" because these cans contain less methyl mercury, due to the various types of tuna used, than "solid" or "chunk white" cans.

SEAFOOD WITH LOW MERCURY LEVELS

The seafood considered low in methyl mercury levels include: catfish, crab, flounder and sole, grouper, haddock, lobster, mahi-mahi, perch, oysters, rainbow trout, salmon, sardines, scallops, shrimp, tilapia, and farmed trout.

Six Tips on How to Shop Wisely and Save Money when Buying Organic

Some moms I've spoken with say they don't or can't buy organic foods due to cost and availability. Here are a few ways to make organics more affordable and easy to purchase.

1. Do not always assume organic is more expensive. Look at the prices of conventional and organic products and compare. You may be surprised that on some items, there is little or no difference in price, depending on where and when you buy.

2. Buy in season. These items will be the lowest priced, whether you're shopping at a specialty market or local farmers' market.

3. Grow your own. Even a small window box can yield some organic herbs or tomatoes. Larger areas can accommodate lettuce, strawberries, broccoli, carrots, and more. A garden is also a great classroom and hobby for children and adults alike.

4. Shop at one of the more than twenty-five hundred farmers' markets in the United States. The produce here is as fresh as possible, because the food is usually picked within twenty-four hours of your purchase. This is a great place to check prices with little effort. Becoming a regular shopper and getting to know growers personally is a good way to get the best selection and price.

5. Join a food cooperative. A food co-op is a kind of buyers' club for affordable, fresh, local organic and natural products. It is an actual store where members buy shares of the business to provide the capital necessary to run the store efficiently. You as a member directly influence the kind and variety of products and foods available and also receive a discount in the store. Many co-ops allow you to buy shares by volunteering several hours per week or month.

6. Visit a farm and pick your own produce. Children love to experience something new, especially when it involves dirt and food. According to Community

Organics and
Other Food
Buzzwords

♥

Supported Agriculture (CSA), "Parents had reported that their children started to eat more vegetables after visiting a farm on a school field trip, having experienced for the first time the process of gardening."

Justifying Expense

Eating is an agricultural and political act, as well as a way to educate your senses.

ALICE WATERS

Even though you've shopped wisely and used the tips above, sometimes organic is more expensive. The cost of converting land, growing methods, and raising practices from conventional to organic is expensive. Consider the cost of health and well-being, as well as a decision to support the environment, preserving water resources and preventing agriculture-related problems. The extra cost may outweigh the worry and concern you have of the possibility of harming your family and the environment.

> *I can't be sure that organic foods are better for my family's health. But to me the organic practices just make sense. Why wouldn't I do my best to avoid feeding my son chemicals and pollutants?*
>
> TWO-YEAR-OLD DEREK'S mom

REDUCING HEALTH RISKS

Buying organic reduces health risks that can be attributed to commercial pesticides and herbicides. The Environmental Protection Agency (EPA) considers 60 percent of all herbicides, 90 percent of all fungicides, and 30 percent of all insecticides as potentially cancer causing. No matter how well you wash certain fruits and vegetables there are still remaining traces of potentially harmful chemicals. A report released by the Environmental Working Group entitled *Pesticides in Children's Food* concluded that the greatest contribution to a person's lifetime risk of cancer from pesticide residues occurs during childhood. Babies' bodies are much more vulnerable to pesticides because their brains and immune systems are still in a state of development. Also, pound for pound, babies eat two to four times more fruits and vegetables than adults, and thus are exposed to a higher percentage of possible contaminants if eating conventionally grown produce.

INCREASING HEALTH BENEFITS

A study at the University of California at Davis (my alma mater) shows that organically grown strawberries, corn, and blackberries are richer in cancer fighting antioxidants, sometimes 60 percent more, than the same conventionally grown crops. Other studies have proven the same for organically grown peaches and pears, too.

Researchers theorize that organically grown plants may produce more antioxidants because they have to work harder to fight off pests and disease otherwise killed by pesticides and chemicals.

REDUCING NITRITES

Some fruits and vegetables you'll want to introduce to your child have high levels of nitrites, due to the fertilized soils in which they grow. The nitrite levels also increase when these food items are stored in your refrigerator. Nitrites are difficult on a baby's system because their stomach acidity is too low to properly break them down. Overexposure can cause anemia or encourage oxygen to be displaced into bloodstreams, resulting in rapid breathing and lethargy. Buying these items (see box below) grown organically and eaten fresh, without storing will lessen exposure. If you choose to buy these foods commercially grown, wait until your baby is over eight months old so they can better process the nitrites. Or you can buy these foods in commercially prepared jars, since baby food companies can screen their produce for nitrites.

HIGH NITRITE FOODS

High nitrite produce includes beets, cantaloupe, carrots, green beans, mustard, spinach, strawberries, and turnips.

Supporting the Environment

Nature is not a place to visit, it is home.

GARY SNYDER, American poet

Some EPA-approved pesticides were registered long before these chemicals were linked to cancer and other diseases and many of these are being reevaluated. Organic agriculture is one way to prevent new chemicals from getting into the air, water, soil, and food. Less contamination means more resources for communities to preserve and share.

LIFESTYLE CHOICE

For some consumers the choice to purchase organics is part of an overall lifestyle. Today, organic products are more than just tomatoes. It applies to milk, yogurt, cheese, hot dogs, chicken, eggs, cereals, snacks, and even clothing items. With the USDA regulating the use of the word *organic* and large food manufacturers wanting in on the 20 to 24 percent growth rate of foods in this class, the products are increasing on the supermarket shelves daily.

SUPPORTING LOCAL COMMUNITY

For the visionaries who started the idea of local organic farming, the practice was about more than high-quality food. They wanted to build a community that supports itself and can ask and answer the question, "Where does your food come from?" They believe that buying locally supports a culture of local farm families and helps build a stronger community. If everyone has a stake in the local food supply, then hopefully everyone will take care of the land and feel connected to the community. Throughout the country there are community farms, farmers' markets, and cooperative gardens, where individuals and families work together to grow, eat, and share the fruits of their labor.

FLAVOR

Healthy soil produces healthy plants, which taste better. A ripe, organic tomato picked off the vine will naturally taste better than one that was picked prematurely and "ripened" with chemicals in a warehouse or truck on the way from a faraway farm. Organic produce can have an intensity of flavor that conventional vegetables lack. In part that's because conventional crops are often grown using nitrogen-based fertilizer, which causes fruits and vegetables to absorb more water and thus dilutes the flavor.

A CHANGING MARKET

Food industry marketers predict that as large food processors develop more organic and natural food offerings, grocery stores sell these products, and the public becomes aware of such foods, the price gap between organics and conventional foods will decrease.

Other Buzzwords: GE, GMO, and GEI

GE refers to genetically engineered seeds. These seeds have somehow been altered by science in order to produce more positive results such as bigger size, brighter colors, or sweeter flavor. *GMO* refers to genetically modified organisms and *GEI* refers to genetically engineered ingredients. These foods have some type of ingredient or process that has altered their genetic makeup to exhibit traits that are not naturally theirs.

There have been many articles and concerns written about the long-term health and environmental effects of these modified foods. Many countries such as England have banned these foods. The U.S. government does not yet require labeling of foods grown from genetically engineered seeds, thus the only way you can be sure to avoid them is to buy certified organic products. Many foods are labeled "No GE" or "GMO Free" in an effort to inform the consumer and better position their product.

The food choices are yours to make. Becoming educated about what you are and aren't buying helps with buying decisions that work for your family's budget, health needs, and values.

Chapter 7 ♥

The Beginners:
Four to Six Months

Introduction Map		
FOODS APPROPRIATE	**REASON**	**CONSISTENCY/TEXTURE**
Liquids: Breast milk/ formula	Provides all vitamins and minerals for first six months	
Cereals: iron-fortified rice cereal mixed with breast milk/ formula/water	Easy to digest Least allergic reactions	Very liquid at first Consistency of runny yogurt Spoon food into baby's mouth
Vegetables: yellow vegetables, including sweet potatoes, squashes Fruit purees: ripe banana, apple, pear	Mild tasting Easy to digest	Very smooth and creamy texture, with nothing to chew Spoon food into baby's mouth.

Introducing Solids

The American Pediatric Association recommends introducing solids between four and six months of age. A few large-scale studies suggest that this timing may lower the risk of developing type I diabetes. Feeding your baby solids before four months can trigger an abnormal reaction in his immature immune system. Many mothers are told by well-meaning family members to give baby solids very young in order to get them to sleep through the night. However, feeding a baby solids does not make them sleep any better. It may just coincide with other developments that encourage routine sleeping patterns at this stage. On the other hand, introducing solids later than six months may inhibit the development of a child's palate, as they will not be exposed to enough variety early on. It is best to check with your child's pediatrician to get the green light based upon your own child's needs and development.

HOW MUCH?

In the beginning your baby will eat about one to two teaspoons of cereal or puree, once or twice per day. Although the first few times, when they're getting acquainted with the process, your baby won't swallow much of anything. He is still drinking about twenty-four to thirty-eight ounces of breast milk or formula each day.

READY?

Many parents, me included, look forward to introducing solids and are just waiting for the right time. But when? The biggest cue is that your child will take an active interest in watching you eat, looking at and trying to grab your food. You'll know they're ready when you start to feel guilty eating a meal in front of them.

Babies have a natural reflex in their tongue called a thrust reflex. This is when the tongue thrusts outward to push items out of the mouth. When this reflex is gone, your baby will be able to eat because he can then swallow food. When I began my son, Jonas, on solids at five months, he still had the reflex. I would spoon the food into his mouth and his tongue would flip up, as if he wanted the spoon under his tongue. He was not yet ready to eat. However, he enjoyed thinking he was eating (though it was on his chin and spoon only) and we continued the routine. After about three days, he stopped thrusting his tongue and learned to swallow.

SET?

It is best to keep a log of foods your baby has eaten. It may sound silly, but it is very easy to forget what your baby has tried or not tried. This information can be provided to your doctor in case of illness or reaction. This information can also prove helpful to babysitters and family members who care for your baby. See log example in Appendix B, page 243. Foods will need to be introduced for three to five days in a row to check for any allergic reactions. Then, if a problem arises, it will be easy to determine the offending food.

GO!

This chapter is about first foods. These are most likely single-item fruit and vegetable purees and cereals. In commercially prepared foods, some companies call these "Stage 1" foods. Rice cereal is the most common introductory food in baby's culinary adventure because it's easy to digest and isn't likely to cause allergies. This is best purchased commercially prepared, because these cereals have an extra boost of iron, which your baby needs after six months of age. There are a few brands to choose from, with organic and GMO-free options. The cereal can be mixed with formula, breast milk, or water. Once introduced, the cereal can also be mixed with fruit, vegetable, and meat purees.

Some parents think that children introduced to vegetables before fruits will not have a sweet tooth. Most nutritionist and doctors disagree with this idea. Children will like sweets. There are also many opinions about the order of food items to introduce. Some experts recommend serving vegetables in order of color—lighter yellows to oranges to lighter greens, then dark greens. This suggestion is because lighter-colored foods tend to be milder in flavor; then as your baby's palate matures the food flavors will increase with color intensity.

WHEN TO STOP

No one wants to waste food; however, forcing your child to eat or "finish their plate" is not advised. Before your baby can speak and tell you he's finished eating, he will give you cues. These include: refusing to open his mouth, looking away, becoming agitated, appearing distracted, or squirming in his chair. According to nutritionist Mary Ellen DiPaola, most children can regulate their own appetites in their early stages of eating. If you force children to eat, they may lose the ability to read their own hunger and full signs. Feeding should be enjoyable for baby and parent, in a relaxed atmosphere, and at your child's natural pace and appetite.

FOODS TO AVOID

There are a few reasons to avoid certain foods when introducing solids. The reasons include allergens, food intolerances, family history, special dietary needs (see Chapter 3, Meeting the Needs), nitrite levels (see Chapter 6, Organics), and choking hazards (see Chapter 5, Food Safety). The biggest concern is potential food allergies and intolerances. Symptoms include rash, hives, respiratory problems, diarrhea, gas, and vomiting. Food allergies and intolerances are often linked genetically, so if parents are allergic they should be cautious and delay introducing these foods to children.

Some foods are more likely to cause adverse reactions. Doctors agree these should not be introduced as first foods, but how long to wait is often debated. Some believe these foods should not be introduced until after one year of age, while others, such as Brock Bernsten, M.D., my son's pediatrician, believe some of these foods such as yogurt and wheat, should be introduced between six and eight months of age. Otherwise you may miss an important window of opportunity when children will try new foods. He cautions, however, to give these foods each day for five to seven consecutive days, rather than the typical three- to five-day recommendation.

Nuts and peanuts are a special concern because of the severity of allergy symptoms affecting the upper respiratory system. Less than 1 percent of children and adults have the allergy. However, there are many processed and prepared foods that you may not realize contain nuts, including cookies, crackers, sauces, and ethnic foods. Many nutritionists suggest waiting to introduce nuts and nut butters until your child is two years old or older.

POTENTIAL ALLERGENS

These include: wheat, cow's milk, soy, nuts, shellfish, strawberries, and egg whites.

Caution—Other Potential Hazards

CEREAL IN A BOTTLE

Do not serve cereal mixed with formula from a bottle. There is the possibility of a baby choking when served cereal from a bottle. Also, a baby tends to fill up after eating a certain volume of food. Putting cereal in the milk may give a baby too much cereal and not enough milk, which could lead to a lowered nutritional intake. Finally, cereal in a bottle can promote tooth decay.

MILK AND HONEY

Never feed a child less than one year old honey. Honey has natural botulism spores that cannot be tolerated by a baby's immature system. The American Academy of Pediatrics also advises against giving babies under one year cow's milk. Many people are confused about this warning because many formulas are milk-based, and yogurt and cheeses are enjoyed by babies younger than one year. Milk is an iron inhibitor, and babies at this stage need lots of iron. While there is milk in yogurt and cheese, it is not as large a quantity as in milk consumed by the baby, so the amount of iron lost when eating these foods is minimal.

PROCESSED FOODS

Additives allow for longer shelf lives, ripened and shiny produce, sweetened snacks, fewer calories, and the list goes on and on. Much is unknown about the long-term effects of additives and preservatives on small children or adults. Processed foods may also have nitrites and nitrosamines, which are known to cause cancer. Processed crackers, cookies, cereals, and cakes often have partially hydrogenated oils, which form trans fats and are believed to cause cardiovascular disease and diabetes. See Chapter 3 to learn about reading labels on processed foods to make informed choices.

THE REST . . .

Other items that should be avoided during a child's early development are caffeine, alcohol, salt, refined sugars, and sodas.

The Beginners: Recipes

Apple Puree

Apples are a great first food because of their sweetness and versatility. Besides being for baby, this puree can be used in all kinds of recipes. Use it to sweeten baked goods, as a topping for pancakes, or even to dress up grilled meats.

Golden and Red Delicious, as well as Fuji apples have the least amount of acid, and thus are the most tolerable for babies. You may peel apples before or after cooking. Cooking with skins on allows the apples to retain more nutrients.

MAKES 4 SERVINGS

6 medium (2- to 3-ounce) organic red delicious apples, quartered and cored just before cooking

Steamer Method: Place prepared apples in a steamer basket set in a pot filled with about 1 to 2 inches of lightly boiling water. Do not let water touch fruit. Cover tightly for best nutrient retention and steam for 10 to 12 minutes or until apples are tender. Apples should pierce easily with a toothpick. Set apples and cooking liquid aside to cool.

Scrape apples to remove skin and puree in a food processor with a steel blade. Add 1 or 2 tablespoons of reserved cooking liquid to make the puree smoother and adjust consistency.

Microwave Method: Place prepared apple quarters in a microwave-safe dish. Add ¼ cup water and cover tightly, allowing a corner to vent. Microwave on High for 3 minutes and stir apples. Re-cover and cook for 3 to 6 minutes, or until tender. Check for doneness, cool, and proceed with directions above.

TIP

An apple a day. When baby is ready for more texture, chunks of steamed apple make a good finger food. If your baby is teething, put steamed apple slices in a freezer bag in the freezer for a soothing treat.

NUTRITION FACTS

Serving Size: ½ cup (113g)

Calories 50
Calories from Fat 0
Total Fat 0g
Saturated Fat 0g
Cholesterol 0mg
Sodium 0mg
Total Carbohydrate 13g
Dietary Fiber 1g
Sugars 11g
Protein 0g

The Beginners:
Four to Six
Months

♥

Apricot Puree

Apricots have a mild yet sweet flavor that is appealing to babies. Besides being enjoyed on its own, apricot puree can lend sweetness to combination purees such as chicken and broccoli.

MAKES 3 SERVINGS

6 large (2- to 3-ounce) organic apricots, halved and pitted

Steamer Method: Place apricots in a steamer basket set in a pot filled with about 1 to 2 inches of lightly boiling water. Be sure water does not touch fruit. Cover tightly for best nutrient retention, and steam for 2 to 3 minutes or until apricots are soft and pierce easily with a toothpick, but not falling apart. Set apricots and cooking liquid aside to cool.

Peel flesh from skin with a spoon or your fingers and puree in a food processor with a steel blade until smooth. No additional liquid should be necessary.

Microwave Method: Place apricots in a microwave-safe dish. Cover tightly, allowing a corner to vent. Microwave on High for 1 minute and stir apricots. Re-cover and cook for 1 to 2 minutes, or until tender. Check for doneness, cool, and proceed with directions above.

TIP

Apricot alert. Apricots are very fragile. Ripen in a sealed plastic or paper bag at room temperature. Pick apricots that are dark yellow or yellow-orange in color and firm, without any bruises or spots.

NUTRITION FACTS

Serving Size: ½ cup (113g)

Calories   50
Calories from Fat   0
Total Fat   0g
Saturated Fat   0g
Cholesterol   0mg
Sodium   0mg
Total Carbohydrate   13g
Dietary Fiber   2g
Sugars   10g
Protein   2g

Asian Pear Puree

Asian pears look more like an apple than a pear, and that's why they're also called "nashi apple." There are Chinese, Japanese, and Asian varieties. The color ranges from light green to brownish-yellow. Inside they are sweet, juicy, and very refreshing.

MAKES 3 SERVINGS

3 medium (3- to 4-ounce) organic Asian pears, quartered and cored just before cooking

Steamer Method: Place prepared pears in a steamer basket set in a pot filled with about 1 to 2 inches of lightly boiling water. Do not let water touch fruit. Cover tightly for best nutrient retention and steam for 10 to 12 minutes or until pears are tender. Pears should pierce easily with a toothpick. Set pears and cooking liquid aside to cool.

Scrape pears to remove skin and puree in a food processor with a steel blade. Add 1 or 2 tablespoons of reserved cooking liquid to puree to add smoothness and adjust consistency.

Microwave Method: Place prepared pear quarters in a microwave-safe dish. Add ¼ cup water and cover tightly, allowing a corner to vent. Microwave on High for 3 minutes and stir pears. Re-cover and cook for 3 to 6 minutes or until tender. Check for doneness, cool, and proceed with directions above.

A NOSE KNOWS!

Regular pears are ripe when the fruit begins to soften. However, Asian pears can be ripe even if very firm. Ripeness is determined by a strong, sweet smell.

NUTRITION FACTS

Serving Size: ½ cup (113g)

Calories 50
Calories from Fat 0
Total Fat 0g
Saturated Fat 0g
Cholesterol 0mg
Sodium 0mg
Total Carbohydrate 12g
Dietary Fiber 4g
Sugars 8g
Protein 1g

The Beginners:
Four to Six
Months
♥

Avocado Puree

Ounce for ounce, avocados contain more folate than other fruits. Avocados are also the highest fruit source of potassium, which helps balance the body's electrolytes, and aids muscle activity, nerve function, and energy metabolism, which helps babies and children grow. Avocados, like bananas, require little effort for a first food, as there is no cooking or processing equipment needed.

MAKES ABOUT ¾ CUP

1 large ripe avocado

Cut avocado lengthwise and remove pit. Scrape avocado flesh from skin with a spoon into a small glass bowl. Mash avocado flesh with a fork (about 1 cup mashed). You may want to add 1 to 2 tablespoons water, breast milk, or formula to thin.

VIVA AVOCADO!

The next time you're making guacamole, save a few slices of avocado for baby. For those who can handle it, cut avocado spears make a good (but slippery) finger food.

For adults, mashed avocado can be mixed with cottage cheese or cream cheese for a nutritious dip for vegetables or high-protein sandwich spread.

---

the
petit
appetit
COOKBOOK
♥

Butternut Squash Puree

Butternut squash is a winter squash, which is actually part of the gourd family. Because of their hard, thick skin they are less fragile than summer squashes. However, given their size and shape they can be difficult to cut, so use caution.

MAKES 5 SERVINGS

1 (1¼-pound) organic butternut squash

Oven Method: Preheat oven to 375°F. Cut squash into quarters; remove seeds and place cut side down in a baking pan. Pour ¼ cup water in bottom of pan. Bake squash until fork tender, about 45 minutes. Remove from oven and scoop out flesh.

Puree the squash after cooking, until you've reached the desired consistency. You may want to add 1 to 2 tablespoons water, breast milk, or formula to thin.

Microwave Method: Cut squash into quarters (this may be difficult, depending on size) and scoop out seeds. Place squash, skin side down, in a microwave-safe dish. Add 1 to 2 tablespoons of water and cover tightly, allowing one corner to vent. Microwave on High for 10 to 12 minutes. Check for doneness, cool, and proceed with directions above.

TIP
For older babies, cut squash flesh into chunks that he can pick up and eat himself.

NUTRITION FACTS
Serving Size: ½ cup (113g)

Calories 45
Calories from Fat 0
Total Fat 0g
Saturated Fat 0g
Cholesterol 0mg
Sodium 0mg
Total Carbohydrate 12g
Dietary Fiber 3g
Sugars 2g
Protein 1g

The Beginners:
Four to Six
Months

♥

Jonas's Acorn Squash Puree

This is named after my son because it was his first solid food after rice cereal. I made a creamy soup for my husband and me, so we all had our squash together. Squash is usually best cooked in the oven to bring out the rich nutty flavor; however, the microwave works great for quick and nutritious steaming. For a hearty soup for the rest of the family, add garlic, cilantro and/or dill, and cream or milk for desired consistency.

MAKES 3 SERVINGS

1 medium (about 1½-pound) organic acorn squash

Oven Method: Preheat oven to 350°F. Pierce squash with a fork 3 or 4 times. Bake squash on a foil-lined pan for 45 to 60 minutes (turning every 25 minutes), or until squash pierces easily with a fork. Cut squash in half and remove seeds.

When squash is cool enough to touch, peel off outer skin. Puree in a food processor or blender fitted with a steel blade. Usually no additional liquid is needed.

Microwave Method: Cut squash in quarters (this may be difficult, depending on size) and scoop out seeds. Place squash, skin side down, in a microwave-safe dish. Add 1 to 2 tablespoons water and cover tightly, allowing one corner to vent. Microwave on High for 10 to 12 minutes. Check for doneness, cool, and proceed with directions above.

THE IOWA QUEEN?

Acorn squash is also known as a table queen or a Des Moines; however, it is the ribbed acornlike shape that gives this winter squash its nickname.

NUTRITION FACTS

Serving Size: ½ cup (113g)

Calories 40
Calories from Fat 0
Total Fat 0g
Saturated Fat 0g
Cholesterol 0mg
Sodium 0mg
Total Carbohydrate 10g
Dietary Fiber 3g
Sugars 0g
Protein 1g

the
petit
appetit
COOKBOOK
♥

Mango Puree

Mangos can be very soft and mushy or on the hard and fibrous side. If you get a good soft and sweet one, there is no need to cook; simply mash like a banana. If the fruit has not ripened when you're ready to use it, steam following the directions below.

MAKES 3 SERVINGS

1 medium (about 12-ounce) organic mango

Carefully carve flesh from pit in center of mango. Cut mango into equal-size chunks.

Steamer Method: Place prepared mango in a steamer basket set in a pot filled with about 1 to 2 inches of lightly boiling water. Do not let water touch fruit. Cover tightly for best nutrient retention and steam for 4 to 6 minutes, depending on ripeness, or until mango is tender. Remove fruit from heat and cool until able to handle.

Remove peel and puree in a food processor with a steel blade until smooth. Additional liquid is not usually needed.

Microwave Method: Cut into equal-size pieces. Place in a microwave-safe dish. Add 1 to 2 tablespoons of water and cover tightly, allowing one corner to vent. Microwave on High for 2 to 5 minutes, depending on ripeness. Check for doneness, cool, and proceed with directions above.

TIP
Older babies can enjoy peeled chunks of mango dipped in yogurt. Adults can enjoy mango in chutneys and salsas to accompany pork and fish dishes.

NUTRITION FACTS

Serving Size: 1/2 cup (113g)

Calories 70
Calories from Fat 0g
Total Fat 0g
Saturated Fat 0g
Cholesterol 0mg
Sodium 0mg
Total Carbohydrate 19g
Dietary Fiber 2g
Sugars 17g
Protein 1g

The Beginners:
Four to Six
Months

♥

Nectarine Puree

The nectarine got its start in China as a genetic variant of the common peach. One Chinese emperor was so enthralled with nectarines that he and his people referred to them as the "nectar of the gods."

MAKES 4 SERVINGS

4 large (4- to 6-ounce), organic nectarines, pitted and cut into
    quarters

Steamer Method: Place prepared nectarines in a steamer basket set in a pot filled with about 1 to 2 inches of lightly boiling water. Do not let water touch fruit. Cover tightly for best nutrient retention and steam for 3 to 5 minutes, or until nectarines are tender, and pierce easily with a toothpick. Set nectarines and cooking liquid aside to cool.

Peel nectarine flesh from skin with a spoon or paring knife, and puree in a food processor with a steel blade, until smooth. Additional liquid is not usually needed.

Microwave Method: Place prepared nectarine quarters in a microwave-safe dish. Microwave on High for 2 minutes, stir and check nectarines and cook for 1 more minute, if necessary. Check for doneness, cool, and proceed with directions above.

NUTRITION FACTS

Serving Size: ½ cup (113g)

Calories 60
Calories from Fat 0
Total Fat 0g
Saturated Fat 0g
Cholesterol 0mg
Sodium 0mg
Total Carbohydrate 13g
Dietary Fiber 2g
Sugars 10g
Protein 1g

Peach Puree

Babies love the sweet taste of peaches. Choose any variety of peach for this puree, as long as they are fresh and ripe. Because ripe peaches are usually so juicy, they will steam quickly, so keep an eye on them to prevent them turning to mush.

MAKES 4 SERVINGS

4 medium (4- to 5-ounce) organic peaches, pitted and cut into equal-size pieces

Steamer Method: Place prepared peaches in a steamer basket set in a pot filled with about 1 to 2 inches of lightly boiling water. Do not let water touch fruit. Cover tightly for best nutrient retention and steam for 2 to 4 minutes or until peaches are tender. Peaches should pierce easily with a toothpick. Set peaches and cooking liquid aside to cool.

Peel peach flesh from skin with a spoon or paring knife, and puree in a food processor with a steel blade, until smooth.

Microwave Method: Place prepared peach quarters in a microwave-safe dish. Microwave on High for 2 minutes. Stir and check peaches and cook for 1 minute, if necessary. Check for doneness, cool, and proceed with directions above.

TIP
Give me a P! Fruits that start with the letter *P*, such as peaches, pears, plums, and prunes, are helpful to ease baby's constipation.

NUTRITION FACTS
Serving Size: 1/2 cup (113g)

Calories 45
Calories from Fat 0
Total Fat 0g
Saturated Fat 0g
Cholesterol 0mg
Sodium 0mg
Total Carbohydrate 11g
Dietary Fiber 2g
Sugars 10g
Protein 1g

The Beginners:
Four to Six
Months
♥

Pear Puree

Pears are usually a pleasing first food to baby, because of their sweet, mild flavor and creamy texture. There are more than three thousand known pear varieties grown around the world, but only a handful have been cultivated into the fruit we enjoy. Luckily you don't need to know about all three thousand! Any variety, such as Anjou, Comice, or Bosc, will work for steaming as long as they are ripe.

MAKES 4 SERVINGS

4 medium (3- to 4-ounce) organic pears, quartered and cored just before cooking

Steamer Method: Place prepared pears in a steamer basket set in a pot filled with 1 to 2 inches of lightly boiling water. Do not let water touch fruit. Cover tightly for best nutrient retention and steam for 10 to 12 minutes, or until pears are tender. Pears should pierce easily with a toothpick. Set pears and cooking liquid aside to cool.

Scrape flesh from skin and puree in a food processor with a steel blade. Add reserved cooking liquid by tablespoons to puree to make smoother and adjust consistency.

Microwave Method: Place prepared pear quarters in a microwave-safe dish. Add ¼ cup water and cover tightly, allowing a corner to vent. Microwave on High for 3 minutes and stir pears. Re-cover and cook for 3 to 6 minutes, or until tender. Check for doneness, cool, and proceed with directions above.

TIP

Did you know that pears are one of the few fruits that do not ripen successfully on the tree? They are harvested by hand when they reach full maturity but before they are ripe. Choose a pear that is bright and fresh looking with no bruises or external damage. Test for ripeness by pressing gently near the stem; if it gives to gentle pressure it is sweet, juicy, and ready to eat.

Plum Puree

There are many varieties of black plums including Black Amber, Burgundy, Catalina, Friar, and Nubiana. All have a dark skin and sweet and juicy flesh. Plums are ripe when they give off an aroma and are soft to the touch. Like peaches, plums steam quickly so stay nearby.

MAKES 4 SERVINGS

6 medium (3- to 4-ounce) organic black plums, halved and pitted

Steamer Method: Place plums in a steamer basket set in a pot filled with 1 to 2 inches of lightly boiling water. Do not let water touch fruit. Cover tightly for best nutrient retention and steam for 2 to 3 minutes or until plums are soft. Plums should pierce easily with a toothpick, but not fall apart. Set plums and cooking liquid aside to cool.

Peel flesh from skin with a spoon or your fingers, and puree in a food processor with a steel blade until smooth. No additional liquid should be necessary.

Microwave Method: Place plums in a microwave-safe dish. Cover tightly, allowing a corner to vent. Microwave on High for 1 minute and stir plums. Re-cover and cook for 1 to 2 minutes or until tender. Check for doneness, cool, and proceed with directions above.

ONLY SKIN DEEP

Plums' long-known "fiber" effect on the body is caused by a substance in the skin. If you peel a plum, it will lose this fiber side effect, while still providing a nutritional treat.

NUTRITION FACTS

Serving Size: 1/2 cup (113g)

Calories 50
Calories from Fat 0
Total Fat 0g
Saturated Fat 0g
Cholesterol 0mg
Sodium 0mg
Total Carbohydrate 13g
Dietary Fiber 2g
Sugars 11g
Protein 1g

The Beginners:
Four to Six
Months

♥

Pluot Puree

Plu what? Pluots, a unique hybrid of around 70 percent plum and 30 percent apricot, was developed in California. This hybrid is really the best of both fruits. The science behind its creation is a closely guarded secret.

MAKES 4 SERVINGS

6 (3- to 4-ounce) organic pluots, halved and pitted

Steamer Method: Place pluots in a steamer basket set in a pot filled with 1 to 2 inches of lightly boiling water. Do not let water touch fruit. Cover tightly for best nutrient retention and steam for 2 to 3 minutes, or until pluots are soft. Pluots should pierce easily with a toothpick, but not fall apart. Set pluots and cooking liquid aside to cool.

Peel flesh from skin with a spoon or your fingers, and puree in a food processor with a steel blade until smooth. No additional liquid should be necessary.

Microwave Method: Place pluots in a microwave-safe dish. Cover tightly, allowing a corner to vent. Microwave on High for 1 minute and stir pluots. Re-cover and cook for 1 to 2 minutes, or until tender. Check for doneness, cool, and proceed with directions above.

NUTRITION FACTS

Serving Size: ½ cup (113g)

Calories   60
Calories from Fat   5
Total Fat   0.5g
Saturated Fat   0g
Cholesterol   0mg
Sodium   0mg
Total Carbohydrate   12g
Dietary Fiber   1g
Sugars   6g
Protein   0g

the
petit
appetit
COOKBOOK
♥

Prune Puree

Prunes are packed with fiber; that's why they are a natural laxative. Your doctor may recommend prune or prune juice for baby's constipation. Feed a small amount as a little will go a long way. Reserve cooking water from prunes and give to baby in a cup or bottle. Freeze juice into cubes to have on hand when your baby has a need.

MAKES 4 SERVINGS

8 medium naturally dried organic prunes (about 1 cup), pitted
1½ cups water

Stovetop Method: Place prunes and water in a small saucepan and boil over medium heat. Reduce heat and cover tightly for best nutrient retention and simmer for 8 to 10 minutes, or until tender. Remove fruit from heat and cool until able to handle.

Puree prunes in a food processor with a steel blade. Add cooking liquid to adjust consistency.

Microwave Method: Place prunes in a microwave-safe dish. Add 2 to 3 tablespoons of water and cover tightly, allowing one corner to vent. Microwave on High for 1 to 2 minutes. Check for doneness, cool, and proceed with directions above.

TIP
Chose prunes that are naturally sun-dried and not treated with sulfur dioxide or paraffin. You can buy naturally dried prunes at farmers' markets, health food stores, and specialty markets.

NUTRITION FACTS
Serving Size: ½ cup (113g)

Calories 200
Calories from Fat 0
Total Fat 0g
Saturated Fat 0g
Cholesterol 0mg
Sodium 10mg
Total Carbohydrate 54g
Dietary Fiber 7g
Sugars 29g
Protein 2g

The Beginners:
Four to Six
Months

♥

Summer Squash Puree

Summer squash varieties include patty pan, crookneck, and sunburst. These squash are yellow and green and have thin, tight skins, which are edible. These have high water content and will create a very liquid puree. You may want to adjust the texture by adding baby's cereal.

MAKES 4 SERVINGS

3 large organic summer squash, cut into 1-inch-thick rounds (about 4 cups)

Steamer Method: Place prepared squash in a steamer basket set in a pot filled with about 1 to 2 inches of lightly boiling water. Do not let water touch squash. Cover tightly for best nutrient retention and steam for 7 to 9 minutes, or until squash is tender. Squash should pierce easily with a toothpick.

Squash does not need to be peeled. Puree in a food processor with a steel blade. Additional liquid is not usually needed.

Microwave Method: Place prepared squash in a microwave-safe dish. Add ¼ cup water and cover tightly, allowing a corner to vent. Microwave on High for 3 minutes, or until tender. Check for doneness, cool, and proceed with directions above.

TIP

Don't be fooled by the name. Some of the summer squash are available all year round.

NUTRITION FACTS

Serving Size: ½ cup (113g)

Calories 25
Calories from Fat 0
Total Fat 0g
Saturated Fat 0g
Cholesterol 0mg
Sodium 0mg
Total Carbohydrate 5g
Dietary Fiber 2g
Sugars 3g
Protein 1g

the
petit
appetit
COOKBOOK
♥

Sweet Pea Puree

Give peas a chance! Many children's first foray into green vegetables is peas, be-cause of their sweet flavor. Just be careful not to overcook. They should be bright green, to preserve the high levels of vitamins A and C, not drab and gray like the jarred version.

MAKES 3 SERVINGS

1 (10-ounce) package frozen organic peas, or 10 ounces shelled fresh
    peas

Steamer Method: Place frozen or fresh peas in a steamer basket set in a pot filled with about 1 to 2 inches of lightly boiling water. Do not let water touch peas. Cover tightly for best nutrient retention and steam for 2 to 3 minutes, or until peas are tender and bright green. Rinse peas in cold water to stop cooking.

Puree in a food processor with a steel blade. Add 1 to 2 tablespoons of reserved cooking liquid to make puree smoother and adjust consis-tency.

Microwave Method: Place frozen or fresh peas in a microwave-safe dish. Add 2 tablespoons water and cover tightly, allowing a corner to vent. Microwave on High for 1 minute and stir peas. Re-cover and cook for 1 minute, or until tender and bright. Cool peas and proceed with directions above.

TIP
Sweet and available! Save yourself time and energy and buy your peas in the freezer section. This way there's no shucking shells. Also they'll be sweet and available all year round.

NUTRITION FACTS

Serving Size: 1/2 cup (113g)

Calories 90
Calories from Fat 0
Total Fat 0g
Saturated Fat 0g
Cholesterol 0mg
Sodium 125mg
Total Carbohydrate 16g
Dietary Fiber 5g
Sugars 6g
Protein 6g

The Beginners:
Four to Six
Months

♥

the
petit
appetit
COOKBOOK
♥

Sweet Potato Puree

I never met a baby who didn't love sweet potatoes. They are much sweeter in taste and higher in nutrients than the basic white potato. They pack more beta carotene (an antioxidant) than any other vegetable and are loaded with fiber and vitamin A. Baking the potatoes in the oven may take longer but the flavor is much richer than steaming in the microwave or stovetop.

MAKES 4 SERVINGS

2 medium (7- to 8-ounce) organic sweet potatoes
Water, formula, or milk

Oven Method: Preheat oven to 425°F. Prick potatoes with a small knife, and place on a baking sheet. Bake for 45 to 60 minutes, or until tender, and skin is wrinkled. Potatoes should pierce easily with a toothpick. Set potatoes aside to cool before handling.

Using your fingers, peel potato skin from flesh. Mash with a fork for thicker potatoes, or puree in a food processor with a steel blade until mashed. For a smoother and less sticky texture, add 1 to 2 tablespoons of water, formula or milk, at a time. Add liquid and process until you've reached desired consistency.

Microwave Method: Prick potatoes with a knife and place potatoes in a microwave-safe dish. Add 1/4 cup water and cover tightly, allowing a corner to vent. Microwave on High for 3 minutes and turn potatoes over. Re-cover and cook for 3 to 6 minutes, or until tender. Check for doneness, cool, and proceed with directions above.

TIP

It's all in the name. The names sweet potatoes and yams are used interchangeably in the United States, although true yams are different from sweet potatoes. Only sweet potatoes can be found in the U.S. You will notice different varieties (with varying shades of orange) in stores, most common are Jewel and Garnet.

Zucchini Puree

Zucchini is a member of the squash family. It ranges in color from dark to light green and is generally four to eight inches in length, although some homegrown "zukes" can reach up to two feet in length and six inches in diameter!

MAKES 3 SERVINGS

2 large organic zucchini, cut into 1-inch-thick rounds (about 4 cups)

Steamer Method: Place prepared zucchini in a steamer basket set in a pot filled with 1 to 2 inches of lightly boiling water. Do not let water touch zucchini. Cover tightly for best nutrient retention and steam for 5 to 7 minutes or until zucchini is tender. Zucchini should pierce easily with a toothpick.

Zucchini does not need to be peeled. Puree in a food processor with a steel blade. Additional liquid is not usually needed.

Microwave Method: Place prepared squash in a microwave-safe dish. Add ¼ cup water and cover tightly, allowing a corner to vent. Microwave on High for 3 minutes, or until tender. Check for doneness, cool, and proceed with directions above.

TIP
Liquid puree? Zucchini, as well as other summer squash, has a high water content, which is released when cooked. This may create a runny puree. To thicken, simply stir in a little of your baby's dry cereal.

NUTRITION FACTS

Serving Size: ½ cup (113g)

Calories   15
Calories from Fat   0
Total Fat   0g
Saturated Fat   0g
Cholesterol   0mg
Sodium   0mg
Total Carbohydrate   3g
Dietary Fiber   1g
Sugars   2g
Protein   1g

The Beginners:
Four to Six
Months

♥

Chapter 8

The Explorers: Six to Nine Months

WHAT KIND OF TEXTURE?

Cereal will be thicker, like oatmeal. Purees will be enjoyed smooth in the beginning of this stage and then become chunkier. To create more texture to foods rather than making smooth purees, pulse the processor on and off until desired consistency is achieved, rather than leaving the processor running.

HOW MUCH?

Babies may now be eating about one-fourth cup of food at each meal, and drinking about twenty-eight to thirty-eight ounces of breast milk or formula. Be sure to offer water to your baby at mealtimes and throughout the day. Many doctors and nutritionists caution parents about serving juice, as it can make your child feel full and thus displace other foods and nutrients. Some recommend diluting 100 percent juice with water. The American Academy of Pediatrics recommends pasteurized juices only and no more than four ounces per day. Offering orange segments is better nutritionally than giving orange juice, as your child will get fiber and other nutrients from the fruit that are missing from the juice.

Introduction Map

(Can eat all Beginners' food, plus the following)

FOODS APPROPRIATE	REASON	CONSISTENCY/TEXTURE
Liquids: Breast milk/formula, water, diluted juice	Provides all vitamins and minerals for first six months. After six months still a valuable source of vitamins, nutrients, and fats needed for development.	
Cereals: oat and barley or multigrain	Need for iron increases as breast milk no longer provides enough.	More texture than Beginners. Cereal is more oatmeal-like.
Vegetable purees: orange and light green vegetables, zucchini, carrots, peas, green beans Fruit purees: peaches, plums	Providing vitamin C rich foods with cereal increases iron absorption	Purees can be a bit chunkier, or make some smooth and cut in small cooked chunks for variety. Spoon food into baby's mouth.
Dairy: plain whole milk yogurt, cottage cheese, ricotta cheese Protein: chicken, lean meats	Need for calcium, fat, and protein for growth, energy, development	Can combine purees with soft cheeses and yogurt to create smooth and consistency. Spoon food into baby's mouth.

READY?

Babies who have mastered basic purees now want a bit more texture and flavor. They are more adept at chewing and swallowing. You will also notice your baby picking up pieces of food. At this stage they will palm and push items with their hands, until they develop a pincer grasp. Let them develop this skill, but realize they may get more on their bibs than in their mouths. Remember, you have more control over your child's diet if you are still feeding them, so stay close and spoon most foods, but allow them to try to pick up and self-feed others.

SET?

As a way of discovering new textures, tastes, and objects, at this stage babies like to put everything in their mouths. Many people think this is a golden opportunity to provide children with as much of a variety of foods, flavors, and textures as possible. They may still enjoy some purees, but you can also create the same favorite foods with texture. Besides using the processor, you'll be mashing, cutting, and chopping to give a variety of textures.

GO!

This chapter has recipes for more intermediate purees, and those foods that were avoided as first-food introductions. In commercially prepared baby foods, these foods are considered "Stage 2." Some of these foods are called combination foods as they have two or more ingredients, mixed, cooked, and/or processed together. You can create your own combinations by cooking and processing foods together or mix together prepared purees. You may want to introduce a strong flavor with a familiar favorite, such as spinach with pear, or cauliflower and sweet potato.

If giving a combination food, be sure you've already successfully introduced all ingredients but one, so you can still watch for allergies and intolerances with new foods. Offer a variety of foods at each meal to keep your child's interest and palate developing.

CAUTION: TEETHING

Most babies are usually cutting teeth at this stage as well. You may be able to feel swelling in the gums, which may bother baby. First look for the front lower two, then front upper two, or eye teeth. The teeth do not necessarily signal they are ready for more advanced solids. Babies will still gum their food, so texture should be soft and easy to chew and swallow. Babies may also need something to suck and chew on to comfort the pressure of teething. You may notice your baby chewing the end of his rubber spoon while eating. Some babies like cold teething rings and washcloths, while others find relief in dad's fingers, pacifiers, or frozen bagels.

You'll find recipes for foods including frozen pieces of fruit, breadsticks, and baby biscotti that may provide relief for teething discomfort.

Dr. Jon Orinstil, D.D.S., recommends practicing dental health with your baby as soon as the first tooth erupts, by wiping those new teeth with a gauze or washcloth to remove food buildup. At age one, a soft child's toothbrush will clean teeth and promote good brushing habits. The first trip to the dentist is not until age three.

The Explorers: Recipes

Kasha Cereal

This is another cereal option to add variety and other grains to your child's breakfast repertoire. Kasha is roasted buckwheat, but despite the name there is no wheat in the grain. Kasha can be purchased in bags or in bulk and sold by the pound.

MAKES 10 SERVINGS

¼ cup uncooked organic kasha
1 cup water, breast milk, or formula

Place kasha in a blender or small food processor fitted with a steel blade and pulverize for 3 to 5 minutes on high speed, or until it is a fine powder. In a small saucepan bring water to a simmer over medium heat. Add kasha and reduce heat to low. Cook 3 to 5 minutes, stirring constantly to stop lumps from forming. If cereal is too thick add 1 to 2 tablespoons of additional liquid while cooking. Kasha can be eaten plain or mixed with any fruit or vegetable puree.

TIP
Create convenience. To have ready-to-cook kasha on hand, pulverize larger quantities in the food processor and store in an airtight container at room temperature. Cooked kasha can also be stored in the freezer for up to one month.

NUTRITION FACTS

Serving Size: 1 ounce (28g)

Calories 15
Calories from Fat 0
Total Fat 0g
Saturated Fat 0g
Cholesterol 0mg
Sodium 0mg
Total Carbohydrate 3g
Dietary Fiber 0g
Sugars 0g
Protein 0g

the
petit
appetit
COOKBOOK
♥

Brown Rice Cereal

Your child's first food will probably be commercially prepared and iron-fortified rice cereal. When your child is older and ready for a new grain, try brown rice. Brown rice is not stripped of its coating, which not only makes it brown, but also more nutritious.

MAKES 1 (1-OUNCE) SERVING

¼ cup uncooked organic brown rice
1 cup water, milk, or formula

Place rice in a blender and pulverize into powder, about 3 to 5 minutes on medium to high speed. Put liquid in a small saucepan and bring to a simmer over medium heat. Stir in brown rice powder and reduce heat to low. Cook for 4 to 5 minutes, whisking constantly to ensure a smooth consistency. If cereal is too thick, add more liquid to reach desired texture.

TIP
Good morning, sweetness. Add a dash of cinnamon to oatmeal and other cereal to wake up baby's taste buds.

NUTRITION FACTS

Serving Size: 1 ounce (284g)

Calories 170
Calories from Fat 10
Total Fat 1.5g
Saturated Fat 0g
Cholesterol 0mg
Sodium 5mg
Total Carbohydrate 36g
Dietary Fiber 2g
Sugars 0g
Protein 4g

The Explorers:
Six to Nine
Months

♥

Vegetable Baby Broth

This recipe is a basic one for a baby's bottle or sippy cup. It delivers a punch of vitamins for a child (or any age) needing a liquid diet or pick-me-up.

These vegetables will be very mushy; however, there's no need to waste them. Reserved vegetables can be mashed or pureed for baby.

MAKES ABOUT 3 CUPS

1 quart cold water

1 cup (3 to 4 ounces) organic cauliflower florets

1 cup (2 to 3 ounces) organic broccoli florets

1 cup organic collard or dandelion greens, rinsed and roughly chopped

1 cup (3 to 4 ounces) organic carrots, cut into rounds

Place water in a medium pot with a lid. Add vegetables and bring to a boil over high heat. Reduce heat to simmer and cover pot. Cook for 1 hour. Strain broth and reserve vegetables. These can be pureed or mashed for baby. Serve warm or cool in a cup or bottle for baby. This broth freezes well in ice cube trays for later use.

TIP

Not just baby broth! This is a great broth for many ages and uses. It can be a liquid meal for someone under the weather, a calcium-rich soup for baby, or a flavorful liquid for poaching meats and fish. Always having broth cubes in the freezer means lots of cooking options for you and your family.

NUTRITION FACTS

Serving Size: ½ cup (113g)

Calories 10
Calories from Fat 0
Total Fat 0g
Saturated Fat 0g
Cholesterol 0mg
Sodium 15mg
Total Carbohydrate 1g
Dietary Fiber 0g
Sugars 1g
Protein 0g

the
petit
appetit
COOKBOOK
♥

Melon-Mango Soup

Soup for breakfast? Packed with vitamins A and C and calcium, this soup makes a great alternative to a plain piece of fruit or a morning shake. The bright sunny color should put a smile on your child's face.

MAKES 3 SERVINGS

½ large organic cantaloupe
½ large organic mango
¾ cup plain organic whole-milk yogurt

Cut cantaloupe in half and remove seeds. Cut flesh away from skin and cut into 1-inch cubes. Peel mango and remove flesh from seed. Cut into 1-inch cubes. Put cantaloupe and mango in a food processor or blender and process until smooth, about 20 seconds. Pour mixture into a large glass or plastic bowl. Stir yogurt into mixture. Cover and chill for 1 hour before serving.

TIP
Mango mania. Mangoes are grown throughout the tropics and are often called "the peach of the tropics." More fresh mangoes are eaten every day than any other fruit in the world.

NUTRITION FACTS

Serving Size: 1 cup (263g)

Calories 120
Calories from Fat 10
Total Fat 1.5g
Saturated Fat 0.5g
Cholesterol 5mg
Sodium 70mg
Total Carbohydrate 24g
Dietary Fiber less than 1g
Sugars 10g
Protein 5g

The Explorers:
Six to Nine
Months
♥

Broccoli or "Little Tree" Puree

No matter how old you are, everyone has referred to broccoli as "little trees." Look for compact heads that are dark green, sage green, or a purple-green color. The floret clusters should be firm, compact, and tightly closed. Avoid bunches that are wilted, shriveled, and those with a pungent odor.

MAKES 3 SERVINGS

1 (1-pound) head organic broccoli, separated into equal-size florets

Steamer Method: Place prepared broccoli in a steamer basket set in a pot filled with about 1 to 2 inches of lightly boiling water. Do not let water touch broccoli. Cover tightly for best nutrient retention and steam for 10 to 12 minutes, or until broccoli is tender. Florets should pierce easily with a toothpick. Immediately transfer steamer basket to sink and run cold water over florets until completely cool, 2 to 3 minutes.

Puree broccoli in a food processor with a steel blade. Additional liquid is not usually needed.

Microwave Method: Place prepared broccoli florets in a microwave-safe dish. Add ¼ cup water and cover tightly, allowing a corner to vent. Microwave on High for 4 minutes and stir broccoli. Re-cover and cook for 4 to 6 minutes, or until tender. Check for doneness, cool, and proceed with directions above.

TIP

Tree, please! For older babies, steam broccoli and serve whole florets by themselves or with your child's favorite dip. Perhaps a nice cheesy sauce (page 120).

NUTRITION FACTS

Serving Size: ½ cup (113g)

Calories 30
Calories from Fat 0
Total Fat 0g
Saturated Fat 0g
Cholesterol 0mg
Sodium 30mg
Total Carbohydrate 6g
Dietary Fiber 3g
Sugars 2g
Protein 3g

the
petit
appetit
COOKBOOK
♥

Cauliflower Puree

Cauliflower is high in vitamins C and B and rich in potassium. The taste is mild and can easily be mixed with other vegetables, such as spinach or broccoli, to mellow the flavor. Cauliflower is available all year round, but is at its peak in late fall and early spring.

MAKES 3 SERVINGS

½ (8- to 9-ounce) head organic cauliflower, separated into equal-size florets

Steamer Method: Place cauliflower in a steamer basket set in a pot filled with about 1 to 2 inches of lightly boiling water. Do not let water touch cauliflower. Cover tightly for best nutrient retention and steam for 10 to 12 minutes, or until cauliflower is tender. Florets should pierce easily with a toothpick. Immediately transfer steamer basket to sink and run cold water over florets until completely cool, 2 to 3 minutes.

Puree in a food processor with a steel blade. Additional liquid is not usually needed.

Microwave Method: Place prepared cauliflower florets in a microwave-safe dish. Add ¼ cup water and cover tightly, allowing a corner to vent. Microwave on High for 4 minutes and stir cauliflower. Re-cover and cook for 4 to 6 minutes, or until tender. Check for doneness, cool, and proceed with directions above.

TIP

Cut the carbs craze. For adults eating fewer carbs, cauliflower is a wonderful alternative to potatoes. Simply puree the cauliflower while still a bit warm, with some butter and Parmesan cheese and you'll have a rich and creamy side dish. Plus, you'll swear you're eating mashed potatoes.

NUTRITION FACTS

Serving Size: ½ cup (113g)

Calories 25
Calories from Fat 5
Total Fat 0.5g
Saturated Fat 0g
Cholesterol 0mg
Sodium 15mg
Total Carbohydrate 5g
Dietary Fiber 3g
Sugars 2g
Protein 2g

The Explorers:
Six to Nine
Months

♥

Cantaloupe Puree

People are always thumping melons in the store. That's because you can hear the seeds rattle inside a juicy cantaloupe. Go ahead and smell the stem end, too. If it's a sweet smell, you've chosen well.

MAKES 4 SERVINGS

1 medium (about 1-pound) organic cantaloupe

Cut cantaloupe into 6 to 8 equal-size pieces. Remove seeds and rind.

Steamer Method: Place prepared melon in a steamer basket set in a pot filled with about 1 to 2 inches of lightly boiling water. Do not let water touch cantaloupe. Cover tightly for best nutrient retention and steam for 3 to 5 minutes, depending on ripeness or until cantaloupe is tender. Remove fruit from heat and cool until able to handle.

Puree in a food processor with a steel blade. No additional liquid will be needed.

Microwave Method: Cut into equal pieces. Place in a microwave-safe dish. Add 1 to 2 tablespoons of water and cover tightly, allowing one corner to vent. Microwave on High for 1 to 2 minutes, depending on ripeness. Check for doneness, cool, and proceed with directions above.

TIP

Wash a cantaloupe? Yes! No, you're not going to eat the skin. However, if there is dirt and bacteria on the outside, you could push it unknowingly into the cantaloupe flesh when it is cut.

NUTRITION FACTS

Serving Size: ½ cup (113g)

Calories 70
Calories from Fat 25
Total Fat 3g
Saturated Fat 1.5g
Cholesterol 5mg
Sodium 170mg
Total Carbohydrate 8g
Dietary Fiber 1g
Sugars 1g
Protein 2g

the
petit
appetit
COOKBOOK
♥

Nice to Meat You

Many parents ask me about cooking meats for their babies. The important things to remember when cooking red meat for baby is to choose lean meat and cook it thoroughly. You can cook any meat your family enjoys—lamb, beef, or veal. Start with ground beef for the easiest texture; then, once baby is ready, simply puree or chop up pieces from your own adult meat cuts for your baby.

MAKES 2 SERVINGS

½ pound lean organic ground beef round
¼ cup water

Heat a nonstick skillet over medium heat. Add beef and water. Cook, breaking up and stirring meat constantly, until meat is cooked and no longer pink, about 5 minutes. Remove from heat and cool. Drain and reserve cooking juices. Transfer meat to a food processor fitted with a steel blade or a blender and puree. Leave processor on 1 to 2 minutes and add cooking juices to adjust consistency. Texture will be pastelike.

TIP
The color of this puree will be less than appetizing. To make a complete meal and also perk up the eye appeal, add baby's favorite vegetable puree such as peas, sweet potatoes, or green beans.

NUTRITION FACTS

Serving Size: ½ cup (113g)

Calories 150
Calories from Fat 70
Total Fat 8g
Saturated Fat 3g
Cholesterol 35mg
Sodium 65mg
Total Carbohydrate 0g
Dietary Fiber 0g
Sugars 0g
Protein 18g

The Explorers:
Six to Nine
Months

♥

NUTRITION FACTS

Serving Size: ½ cup (113g)

Calories 50
Calories from Fat 0
Total Fat 0g
Saturated Fat 0g
Cholesterol 0mg
Sodium 90mg
Total Carbohydrate 11g
Dietary Fiber 3g
Sugars 8g
Protein 2g

the
petit
appetit
COOKBOOK

♥

Baby's Got the Beet

One of my clients used a diaper service that made parents agree not to serve their children beets. The expression "beet red" applies to the color going in and going out, which may stain cloth.

MAKES 4 SERVINGS

4 large (3- to 4-ounces) organic beets, scrubbed

Preheat oven to 350°F. Trim beets of root and tips and pierce skin with a knife. Wrap beets together in foil and place in a baking pan. Bake in oven for 45 to 60 minutes, or until fork tender. Remove beets from oven and let cool. When cool enough to handle peel skin from beets using fingers or paring knife. Puree beets in a food processor fitted with a steel blade. No additional liquid will be required.

Parsnip and Carrot Puree

Parsnips and carrots make a good match because they cook at the same rate and complement each other's flavor. The carrots lend sweetness to the earthiness of the parsnips.

MAKES 4 SERVINGS

3 large organic carrots, or 1-pound bag organic baby carrots, peeled
3 large (1 pound) organic parsnips, peeled

Steamer Method: Place prepared carrots and parsnips together in a steamer basket set in a pot with about 1 to 2 inches of water of lightly boiling water. Do not let water touch vegetables. Cover tightly for best nutrient retention and steam for 10 to 12 minutes or until carrots are tender. Carrots and parsnips should pierce easily with a toothpick. Set aside to cool.

Puree carrots and parsnips together in a food processor with a steel blade. Add tablespoons of reserved cooking liquid to puree to make smoother and adjust consistency.

Microwave Method: Place prepared carrots and parsnips in a microwave-safe dish. Add ¼ cup water and cover tightly, allowing a corner to vent. Microwave on High for 3 minutes and stir. Re-cover and cook for 3 to 6 minutes, or until tender. Check for doneness, cool, and proceed with directions above.

TIP
Combining foods. Once you start to combine foods, you'll realize the flavors and textures you can create are endless. Just be sure baby tastes foods separately first to check for allergies. Also serve some combined and some separate so he learns the true flavor of each item on its own.

NUTRITION FACTS

Serving Size: ½ cup (113g)

Calories 60
Calories from Fat 0
Total Fat 0g
Saturated Fat 0g
Cholesterol 0mg
Sodium 40mg
Total Carbohydrate 15g
Dietary Fiber 3g
Sugars 5g
Protein 1g

The Explorers:
Six to Nine
Months

♥

Green Bean Puree

Green beans are a good vegetable for all ages. There are so many ways you can enjoy them: pureed, steamed, stir-fried, even raw.

MAKES 2 TO 3 SERVINGS

8 ounces organic green beans, tips trimmed off

Steamer Method: Place prepared beans in a steamer basket set in a pot filled with about 1 to 2 inches of lightly boiling water. Do not let water touch beans. Cover tightly for best nutrient retention and steam for 10 to 12 minutes, or until beans are tender. Beans should pierce easily with a toothpick. Immediately transfer steamer basket to sink and run cold water over beans until completely cool, 2 to 3 minutes.

Puree beans in a blender with a steel blade. Add cooking liquid to reach desired consistency.

Microwave Method: Place prepared beans in a microwave-safe dish. Add ¼ cup water and cover tightly, allowing a corner to vent. Microwave on High for 3 minutes and stir beans. Re-cover and cook another 3 minutes, or until tender. Check for doneness, cool, and proceed with directions above.

TIP
It's not easy . . . bean green. Be sure to cook beans until very tender, as they are fibrous and difficult to puree and digest.

NUTRITION FACTS

Serving Size: ½ cup (113g)

Calories   35
Calories from Fat   0
Total Fat   0g
Saturated Fat   0g
Cholesterol   0mg
Sodium   5mg
Total Carbohydrate   8g
Dietary Fiber   4g
Sugars   2g
Protein   2g

the
petit
appetit
COOKBOOK
♥

Carrot Puree

Done correctly, steamed carrots are a beautiful bright orange, which definitely attracts baby to the spoon. Some pediatricians can tell which of their patients enjoy orange vegetables, as an abundance of orange veggies in baby's diet can give baby's skin an orange hue. That orange color in the vegetable (and the baby) comes from beta carotene.

MAKES 4 SERVINGS

6 large organic carrots or about 2 pounds organic baby carrots, peeled and cut into 1½-inch pieces

Steamer Method: Place prepared carrots in a steamer basket set in a pot filled with about 1 to 2 inches of lightly boiling water. Do not let water touch carrots. Cover tightly for best nutrient retention and steam for 10 to 12 minutes or until carrots are tender. Carrots should pierce easily with a toothpick. Set carrots and cooking liquid aside to cool.

Puree carrots in a food processor with a steel blade. Add tablespoons of reserved cooking liquid to puree to make smoother and adjust consistency.

Microwave Method: Place prepared carrots in a microwave-safe dish. Add ¼ cup water and cover tightly, allowing a corner to vent. Microwave on high for 3 minutes and stir carrots. Re-cover and cook for 3 to 6 minutes, or until tender. Check for doneness, cool, and proceed with directions above.

TIPS

Carrot convenience. The organic bags of baby carrots are so simple to use. They're already peeled and the sizes are perfect without cutting. Just remember to wash; even though they look clean—they may not be.

Carrots are high in nitrites, so be sure to feed your family fresh, organic carrots to minimize nitrite levels. Nitrite levels increase the longer the carrots sit. Buy them and eat them; don't age them in your refrigerator.

NUTRITION FACTS

Serving Size: ½ cup (113g)

Calories 40
Calories from Fat 0
Total Fat 0g
Saturated Fat 0g
Cholesterol 0mg
Sodium 65mg
Total Carbohydrate 9g
Dietary Fiber 3g
Sugars 4g
Protein 1g

The Explorers:
Six to Nine
Months

♥

Chicken Puree

Having cooked chicken on hand is a great convenience. Make a few chicken breasts to create puree for Explorers, finger foods for Independents, and salads and sandwiches for Connoisseurs. Cook chicken using the method you're most comfortable with. The oven method gives the most flavor, while poaching yields the most moisture and juice.

MAKES 4 SERVINGS

1 (¾- to 1-pound) cage-free, organic boneless chicken breast

Poaching Method: Heat about ½ inch of water in a medium skillet over medium-high heat until simmering. Add chicken breast. Water should not cover chicken, but come up about halfway. Simmer chicken until opaque and cooked through, 3 to 4 minutes per side.

Remove skin. Coarsely chop chicken and transfer to a food processor. Process chicken for about 1 minute. While processor is running, slowly add ¼ cup of the cooking liquid or water and continue to process into a paste. Add more liquid as needed to reach desired consistency.

Oven Method: Preheat oven to 400°F. Place chicken breast on greased baking rack over baking pan. Bake chicken 12 minutes on each side, or until cooked through.

Microwave Method: Place whole chicken breast in a microwave-safe dish. Add ¼ cup water and cover tightly, allowing a corner to vent. Microwave on High for 5 to 7, or until cooked. Check for doneness, cool, and proceed with directions above.

TIP

Sweet texture. For a creamier texture, add yogurt or another of baby's favorites such as Sweet Pea Puree (page 73) or Apple Puree (page 59) to the chicken puree.

NUTRITION FACTS

Serving Size: ½ cup (113g)

Calories 210
Calories from Fat 80
Total Fat 8g
Saturated Fat 2.5g
Cholesterol 85mg
Sodium 70mg
Total Carbohydrate 0g
Dietary Fiber 0g
Sugars 0g
Protein 31g

the
petit
appetit
COOKBOOK
♥

Red Beans and Rice

Let baby celebrate Mardi Gras with a Southern favorite. Dark red in color, small red beans are smoother in taste and texture than the dark red kidney bean, but use whichever you like.

MAKES 4 SERVINGS

½ cup short-grain uncooked organic white rice
½ cup cooked whole or canned organic red beans, rinsed
2 cups water

In a saucepan, combine rice and water and heat over medium-high heat until boiling. Turn heat to low and simmer, covered, for 40 minutes, or until water is absorbed and rice is cooked. Stir together rice and beans.

Eat beans and rice whole, mash together with a fork, or puree in a food processor with additional water for a coarse puree.

TIP
Cooking dry beans. If using dry beans, boil in a pot with a tight-fitting lid for approximately 1½ hours. If you have a pressure cooker, you can reduce the cooking time to 18 to 25 minutes. One cup of uncooked beans yields approximately 2½ cups cooked.

NUTRITION FACTS

Serving Size: 6 oz (170g)

Calories   120
Calories from Fat   0
Total Fat   0g
Saturated Fat   0g
Cholesterol   0mg
Sodium   0mg
Total Carbohydrate   26g
Dietary Fiber   3g
Sugars   1g
Protein   4g

Brown Rice with Lentils

Rice and legumes are a wonderful combination to make a complete protein for vegetarian and non-vegetarian babies. Lentils, unlike other beans, require little cooking time and are easy to mash for older babies. If you have leftovers of one or both, simply mash or puree to combine. You can even add chopped chicken or mashed vegetables for variety.

MAKES 3 SERVINGS

½ cup short-grain uncooked organic brown rice
½ cup uncooked organic green lentils
2 cups water

In a saucepan combine rice, lentils, and water and heat over medium-high heat until boiling. Turn heat to low and simmer for 40 minutes or until water is absorbed and rice is cooked.

Simply mash with a fork. Or puree in a food processor with additional water for a coarse puree.

TIP

There are many rice options: white, brown, long-grain, short-grain, sticky, basmati, jasmine, and many others. Experiment with different grains and tastes to find your family's favorites. Adjust cooking time 5 to 10 minutes, depending on grain type.

Baby's Beans

Beans are a good source of protein for both vegetarian and meat-eating babies. They are versatile for creating various textures and consistencies, as well as a base for dips, spreads, and soups. Canned beans are more convenient than cooked, but if you have the time, make a large batch to use in multiple recipes. See Tip on page 93 for instructions on cooking beans.

MAKES 16 SERVINGS

1 (16-ounce) can or 1½ cups cooked organic beans (black, kidney, cannelini)
2 tablespoons plain organic whole-milk yogurt

Rinse beans with running water and rub off any bean skins. Put beans and yogurt in a food processor and pulse on and off to create a coarse puree. For a smoother consistency, process longer and add more yogurt. For a more coarse texture, simply mash the beans with a fork and mix with yogurt.

NUTRITION FACTS

Serving Size: 2 tablespoons (30g)

Calories 25
Calories from Fat 0
Total Fat 0g
Saturated Fat 0g
Cholesterol 0mg
Sodium 85mg
Total Carbohydrate 4g
Dietary Fiber 1g
Sugars 0g
Protein 1g

The Explorers:
Six to Nine
Months

♥

WHEAT FREE

NUTRITION FACTS

Serving Size: ¼ of squash
(239g)

Calories 60
Calories from Fat 5
Total Fat 0.5g
Saturated Fat 0g
Cholesterol 0mg
Sodium 40mg
Total Carbohydrate 16g
Dietary Fiber 3g
Sugars 6g
Protein 2g

the
petit
appetit
COOKBOOK

♥

Spaghetti Squash

My mom got a microwave when they first came on the market. It was the seventies and microwaves were large, expensive, and mysterious. Mom and I went to a class to learn how to use it, and spaghetti squash was one of the food items they taught us to prepare. Because of the strands created when cooked, this squash is a perfect pasta alternative topped with sauce (see page 148).

MAKES 4 SERVINGS

1 organic spaghetti squash
¼ cup water
Freshly squeezed lemon juice
Salt and black pepper, to taste

Oven Method: Preheat oven to 350°F. Cut squash in half lengthwise and remove seeds. Place squash halves cut side down in a large baking pan with water, and bake for 45 minutes, or until tender.

Cool slightly. Pull out squash strands with a fork. Eat plain or with lemon juice, salt, and pepper.

Microwave Method: Prepare squash for cooking as above. Place cut side down in glass dish with water and cover with plastic wrap. Cook on High for 7 to 9 minutes, or until tender. Check for doneness, cool, and proceed with directions above.

Baby Biscotti

For those who are not afraid to give their children some sugar, these are a good biscuit for older babies. They are sweet, light and hard, but fall apart easily when chewed. Feel free to shape in whatever size and shape your little one can grab.

MAKES ABOUT 85 PIECES

3 cage-free, organic eggs

2 cups organic confectioner's sugar

1 teaspoon vanilla extract

1 teaspoon baking powder

3 cups unbleached all-purpose flour

Heat oven to 375°F. Beat eggs, sugar, and vanilla with electric mixer on high until batter is thick and pale, 8 minutes. In a separate bowl, combine flour and baking powder. Gradually add flour mixture to egg mixture. Add additional flour if too sticky to shape. Roll dough into smooth balls (about 2 tablespoons each) and shape balls into about 2½-inch-long flat logs on a nonstick baking sheet. Bake for 12 minutes, or until bottoms are lightly browned. Turn off oven. Loosen cookies, but keep cookies on baking sheet in hot oven until cool, 3 to 4 hours or overnight.

Not just for babies! These biscotti make a great adult treat dipped in coffee.

NUTRITION FACTS

Serving Size: 1 biscotti (28g)

Calories 100
Calories from Fat 5
Total Fat 0.5g
Saturated Fat 0g
Cholesterol 20mg
Sodium 20mg
Total Carbohydrate 20g
Dietary Fiber 0g
Sugars 11g
Protein 2g

The Explorers:
Six to Nine
Months

❤

the
petit
appetit
COOKBOOK
♥

First Fish

This is an easy way to prepare fish for your baby or toddler. Because of the mild and "non-fishy" taste, tilapia is a good introduction to seafood for a little one. Fish can be thinned with reserved cooking broth, or mix with plain yogurt or cottage cheese for a more creamy texture.

MAKES 2 SERVINGS

1 cup organic vegetable broth
2 (4-ounce) white fish fillets

Heat broth in a medium skillet over medium-high heat until simmering. Add fish fillets. Broth should not cover fish, but come up about halfway. Simmer fish until opaque, 3 to 4 minutes per side. Fish should flake easily with a fork. Remove fish from pan and mash with a fork to desired consistency, or puree with some of the cooking liquid in a food processor.

TIP

No bones about it. Be sure to check fish carefully for small bones before feeding to baby. Fillets have fewer bones than steaks.

Citrus-Corn Muffins

This savory muffin is inspired from a healthy spa recipe. For adult mouths, bake in regular-size muffin cups and serve as an accompaniment to soups or salads. For smaller mouths and tummies, bake in mini muffin cups and break into tiny bite-size pieces. If using mini muffin pans, reduce baking time to 10 to 12 minutes.

MAKES 18 LARGE MUFFINS OR 36 MINI MUFFINS

2 cups unbleached all-purpose flour

½ cup organic cornmeal

1 tablespoon baking powder

1 teaspoon salt

1 cup low-fat buttermilk

2 large cage-free, organic eggs

½ cup packed organic light brown sugar

½ cup mashed banana (about 1 large organic banana)

1 tablespoon grated orange (2 medium organic oranges)

Preheat oven to 400°F. Lightly grease 12-cup standard muffin pan or 24-cup mini muffin pan with vegetable oil. In a large bowl, whisk together flour, cornmeal, baking powder and salt. In a medium bowl, combine buttermilk, eggs, brown sugar, banana, and zest. Mix well. Using a rubber spatula, fold buttermilk mixture into flour mixture. Be careful not to overmix, as muffins will be tough.

Spoon batter into muffin cups, filling about three-fourths full. Bake for 15 to 20 minutes, or until muffins are brown on top and a wooden pick comes out clean. Remove muffin pan from oven and place on a wire rack to cool. Turn out muffins onto rack to cool completely. If muffins stick to pan, run a dull knife around edge of muffins to release.

TIP

Get picky. Keep toothpicks or small wooden skewers on hand to check muffins and other baked goods for doneness. Simply insert pick in center, and when it comes out clean, muffins are done.

VEGETARIAN

NUTRITION FACTS

Serving Size: 1 large muffin (50g)

Calories 100
Calories from Fat 5
Total Fat 1g
Saturated Fat 0g
Cholesterol 25mg
Sodium 240mg
Total Carbohydrate 21g
Dietary Fiber less than 1g
Sugars 7g
Protein 3g

The Explorers:
Six to Nine
Months

♥

Chapter 9

The Independents: Nine to Twelve Months

Introducing

According to most pediatricians, this is a good time to introduce whole-milk dairy products and hard-cooked eggs. Some doctors recommend eating only egg yolks during the first year, due to potential allergies to egg whites. Unless the eggs are hard-cooked, however, even the most careful person will mix in some egg whites when separating out the yolks, which could cause a problem. Since most foods and recipes use the whole egg, it is difficult to avoid whites. Brock Bernsten, M.D., recommends introducing the whole egg at one time. If your child is allergic to whites, you'll most likely want to avoid eggs in general. Check with your child's pediatrician if you have questions about eggs or if you have a history of egg allergies in your child's family. There are egg-free noodles and processed foods without eggs that can be found in most supermarkets.

HOW MUCH?

By now you've most likely received the go-ahead from your pediatrician to introduce a third daily meal for your child during this time. At each of your child's meals, he may now be eating up to four ounces

Introduction Map

(Can eat all Explorers' food, plus the following)

FOODS APPROPRIATE	REASON	CONSISTENCY/TEXTURE
Liquids: Breast milk/formula, plus water and diluted juice (if desired)	Still a valuable source of vitamins, nutrients, and fats needed for development	
Grains: egg-free pasta, brown rice, and bread	Good source of fiber and carbohydrates	Small pieces of toasted bread and cooked pasta for picking up. Rice mixed with vegetable purees.
Legumes and beans, plus dark-colored vegetables: greens, spinach, beets Fruit: kiwifruit, berries, citrus. Introduce spices.	Good source of vitamins C and D and zinc. Combine grains, legumes, and vegetables to create complex proteins. Spices for variety and expanding palate.	Cut foods into small pieces, as well as continue with mashed and pureed foods for a variety of textures. They will want to use the spoon themselves, and pick up food with fingers.
Dairy and proteins: cooked egg yolk, fish, tofu	Valuable proteins	Mixed meals

or one tablespoon of each food type and drinking twenty-four to thirty-four ounces of breast milk or formula each day.

READY?

You may not be ready for this stage. Things get more messy and loud, as children exert their independence and want to feed themselves and become frustrated if unsuccessful. This includes trying to take the utensils and everything else they can reach off the table. Some parents prefer to eat at home with an Independent child to reduce stress and anxiety. Nine-and-a-half-month-old Jackson's mom says, "We can no longer take Jackson out to dinner. He wants to touch and grab everything and he squeals loudly if we stop him." Other parents are more flexible with meal-time behavior and enjoy family meals at home and restaurants. You'll need to decide what works for you and you family.

> *The worst advice I ever heard was, "Don't let kids play with food." Playing with food makes eating fun. Most parents I know who don't let their kids play with their food (within reason) end up with really picky eaters. Kids are going to want to eat strange food combos, and half the fun for our daughter is dipping pasta into a glass of water, or mixing ketchup with juice, then drinking it. I'm convinced that's why Delilah eats pretty much anything and we've never had food issues.*
>
> THREE-YEAR-OLD DELILAH'S dad

SET?

At the end of this stage and beginning the next, your baby will likely be eating "table foods." These are foods that the rest of the family is eating at mealtimes. Adventurous parents cut small bites from their plates, but more cautious parents are timid to go the next step and remain with purees and cereals, because it is easier for them in terms of mess and control. This may be more difficult in the long run, as it could take your child longer to develop eating and feeding skills, and also inhibit his palate. Other parents take a middle-of-the-road approach and set aside special ingredients from the family meal to prepare separately without heavy spices and sauces.

Your child's new pincer grasp allows him to pick up food and other items between his thumb and other fingers. Children at this stage will be more efficient at feeding themselves with their fingers and may even hold utensils.

GO!

Go at your and your child's own pace. If your baby began his culinary adventure early, he may already have a variety of favorite foods. He may also stop opening his mouth for past favorites. My son refused to eat some of his favorites, such as ricotta cheese and avocado, from his spoon. However, he continued to love those foods if spread on tiny pieces of toast and given with fingers. So you need to be creative and flexible at mealtimes. This chapter has a variety of suggestions for snacks and meals. The recipes include finger foods and those that easily stick to a child's spoon, to encourage and empower the Independent child.

Spice it up! Many parents are afraid to add herbs and spices to children's food. Try introducing sweet or mild herbs and spices first, such as cinnamon, thyme, and rosemary. Then add something bolder, like garlic, basil, or curry powder. You'll be surprised at what wakes up your child's palate. At ten months, my son, Jonas, was enjoying cinnamon on his oatmeal and cumin on his chicken. By one year, flavorful Mexican and Indian dishes were his favorites.

A study by the U.S. Department of Agriculture found that half a teaspoon of cinnamon twice a day reduces the risk of type II diabetes by lowering levels of glucose and cholesterol. Sprinkle it on your child's toast, cereal, fruit, and yogurt for sweetness and health.

CAUTION: CHOKING HAZARDS

I have seen many kids almost die from such choking hazards as hot dogs and gumballs. I never want to tell a family that they've lost their child to such a senseless tragedy.

CYNTHIA SIMMONS, M.D., Emergency Room Pediatrician

At this stage the foods to avoid are those that are a potential choking hazard. Your child is particularly at risk when he is feeding himself. Children often put too much food in their mouths or don't completely chew before swallowing. This is why it is important to watch your child eat. Monitoring the amount of food your child is eating at once is a good idea. According to Mark Altman, The Childproofer, even those friendly cereal Os became a choking hazard when his son packed too many inside his mouth at once. The suggestion is to dole out smaller amounts of food and always be available to give more.

Foods that are a particular choking risk include pieces of hot dogs, nuts, marshmallows, raw carrots and celery, popcorn, grapes, cherries, raisins, pumpkin (pepitas) and sunflower seeds, and peanut butter.

The Independents: Recipes

Mini Banana Apple Bran Muffins

NUTRITION FACTS

Serving Size: 2 mini muffins
(65g)

Calories 160
Calories from Fat 80
Total Fat 9g
Saturated Fat 4g
Cholesterol 55mg
Sodium 270mg
Total Carbohydrate 18g
Dietary Fiber 2g
Sugars 8g
Protein 3g

These mini muffins have all the flavor of a big muffin, but fit nicely into little hands. Of course you can also make these in a regular full-size muffin pan; just remember to increase baking time to 15 to 18 minutes and check for doneness. Be sure you've already introduced wheat and eggs before giving these muffins to baby.

MAKES 24 MINI MUFFINS OR 12 REGULAR MUFFINS

1 cup organic whole wheat flour

½ cup organic oat bran

1 teaspoon baking soda

½ teaspoon salt

½ cup (1 stick) unsalted butter

¾ cup organic applesauce or Apple Puree (page 59)

3 medium organic bananas, 1 mashed (about ½ cup) and 2 sliced

½ cup packed organic light brown sugar

2 cage-free, organic eggs

Preheat oven to 375°F. Grease 24 mini muffin cups or 12 regular muffin cups.

With a fork, combine flour, bran, baking soda, and salt in a small mixing bowl. Melt butter in a small saucepan over low heat or in a microwave for 25 seconds on High. In a large bowl, combine melted butter, applesauce, mashed banana, sugar, and eggs. Mix together with a rubber spatula. Add flour mixture to applesauce mixture and stir until just blended. Batter will be lumpy and very moist.

Spoon batter into prepared muffin cups, filling two-thirds full. Place banana slice on top of each muffin. Bake for 12 minutes, or until golden brown and set. Cool muffins in pan on a wire rack for 5 minutes before turning out muffins.

TIP

Pick a test. Because these muffins are so moist with the mashed bananas and applesauce, the wooden-pick test is difficult. The center may not come out clean if you hit a chunk of banana. If you're not sure if they're done, you can always pop one out and take a taste.

Roasted Herb Chicken

This is an easy weeknight meal, with lots of weeknight leftover possibilities. Cooking an entire chicken provides something for everyone, dark meat, white meat, sliced, or enjoyed right on the bone. You can even puree breast meat for baby.

MAKES 4 SERVINGS

1 (3- to 3½-pound) organic broiler chicken

2 tablespoons olive oil

2 tablespoons freshly squeezed lemon juice

1 teaspoon minced fresh thyme

Preheat oven to 375°F. Rinse chicken and pat dry. Be sure giblets and neck are removed. Place chicken breast-side-up on oiled rack in a shallow roasting pan. In a small bowl, whisk together oil, juice, and thyme. Brush over chicken. Roast chicken, uncovered, for 1¼ to 1½ hours, basting with pan juices halfway through cooking. Cook until flesh is no longer pink and juices run clear.

TIP

What's old is new. In 1950, approximately 80 percent of chickens were free range; by 1980, only 1 percent were free range. Today it is back up to 12 percent.

NUTRITION FACTS

Serving Size: 4 oz (113g)

Calories   510
Calories from Fat   420
Total Fat   46g
Saturated Fat   13g
Cholesterol   90mg
Sodium   70mg
Total Carbohydrate   0g
Dietary Fiber   0g
Sugars   0g
Protein   22g

the
petit
appetit
COOKBOOK
♥

No Yolking Around Pancakes

Jonathan, a two-and-a-half-year-old, was allergic to eggs but wanted to eat pancakes. His mom couldn't find a recipe without eggs, so she sent me a request and challenge: Find an egg-free pancake recipe. I couldn't find one either, so I came up with my own. This allows those not yet introduced to eggs to enjoy pancakes with the rest of the family. These are great with Blueberry Syrup (page 121) and fresh berries.

MAKES ABOUT 8 (5-INCH) PANCAKES; 4 SERVINGS

1 cup organic whole wheat flour

1 tablespoon organic cane sugar

2 teaspoons baking powder

¼ teaspoon salt

½ teaspoon baking soda

½ teaspoon ground cinnamon

1 cup organic milk

2 tablespoons expeller pressed canola oil

In a medium mixing bowl, stir together flour, sugar, baking powder, salt, baking soda, and cinnamon. In a separate bowl, whisk together milk and oil. Add milk mixture to flour mixture all at once. Stir with a rubber spatula until just blended. If batter is too thick, thin with milk.

Heat a large nonstick skillet or griddle over medium heat. Lightly grease skillet with cooking spray or melted butter.

For each pancake, pour about ¼ cup batter onto hot griddle or skillet. Cook until bubbles form on top of pancakes and bottoms are golden and set. Flip with a spatula and brown other sides until golden. Warm finished pancakes in a 300°F oven, while continuing to use batter to make more batches.

TIP

Packing pancakes. Pancakes make a great snack for packing and snacking. Make a double recipe and seal cold, leftover pancakes in a zipper bag in your refrigerator or freezer. They make fast, convenient on-the-go finger foods.

NUTRITION FACTS

Serving Size: 2 pancakes (52g)

Calories 100
Calories from Fat 40
Total Fat 4.5g
Saturated Fat 0.5g
Cholesterol 0mg
Sodium 290mg
Total Carbohydrate 14g
Dietary Fiber 2g
Sugars 2g
Protein 3g

The Independents: Nine to Twelve Months

♥

Curry and Herb Peas

The cumin and curry makes this dish aromatic, but not too spicy for those just trying spices. These peas make a great accompaniment to grilled fish and meats for all ages. Due to the short season for fresh peas and the time required for shucking, I recommend using frozen organic peas.

MAKES 6 TO 7 SERVINGS

1 tablespoon unsalted butter

2 garlic cloves, minced

1 teaspoon curry powder

½ teaspoon ground cumin

⅓ cup water

16 ounces fresh organic peas or 1 (16-ounce) package frozen, organic peas, thawed

½ cup chopped fresh cilantro (optional)

Heat butter in large saucepan over medium heat. When foam subsides, add garlic to pan and quickly sauté until light brown. Stir in curry powder, cumin, water, and peas and simmer until peas are tender and heated through, about 5 minutes. Stir in cilantro, if desired.

TIP

Mind your peas! They will cook quickly. If they are overcooked, they can become mushy and lose their bright color and sweet flavor.

NUTRITION FACTS

Serving Size: 3 oz (85g)

Calories 70
Calories from Fat 20
Total Fat 2g
Saturated Fat 1g
Cholesterol 5mg
Sodium 80mg
Total Carbohydrate 10g
Dietary Fiber 3g
Sugars 4g
Protein 4g

the
petit
appetit
COOKBOOK
♥

Cinnamon Dots or "Lisa Cookies"

My two-year-old friend Emma loved these cookies and every time she saw me she'd say, "Lisa cookies, Lisa cookies." Emma never missed the sugar in this moist cookie and neither will your child. It's the juice and rice syrup that provide the sweet taste.

MAKES ABOUT 50 (1½-INCH) COOKIES

½ cup organic brown rice syrup

¼ cup expeller pressed canola oil

¼ cup organic pineapple juice

½ teaspoon salt

½ teaspoon baking powder

½ teaspoon ground cinnamon

¼ cup organic soy flour

1¼ cups organic brown rice flour

Heat oven to 350°F. Line 2 baking sheets with parchment paper.

Whisk syrup, oil, and juice in a medium bowl. Add remaining ingredients, one at a time, mixing after each addition. Chill dough in refrigerator for 30 minutes. Roll dough with hands into desired-size balls and place on prepared baking sheets. Bake 12 minutes, or until cookies are golden underneath. Use a spatula to transfer cookies to a wire rack to cool.

TIPS

Rice in cookies? Rice syrup and rice flour are good baking alternatives to refined sugars and flours. You can find rice syrup in jars next to molasses on the supermarket shelf. The flour can be purchased in bulk or in bags where organic foods are sold.

Sticky situation. When measuring something sticky like brown rice flour, molasses, or honey, spray a fine mist of oil on the measuring cup or spoon. The sticky ingredient won't stick! Here you can save a step, by measuring the oil before the brown rice syrup and using the same measuring container.

NUTRITION FACTS

Serving Size: 1 cookie (10g)

Calories 40
Calories from Fat 15
Total Fat 1.5g
Saturated Fat 0g
Cholesterol 0mg
Sodium 30mg
Total Carbohydrate 6g
Dietary Fiber 0g
Sugars 2g
Protein 1g

The Independents: Nine to Twelve Months

♥

Blueberry Blend-Up

Blueberries contain a number of vitamins, including A, C, and E, as well as antioxidants that protect the body against chronic diseases associated with the aging process. Be careful if serving blueberries whole, as they can be a choking hazard to young children.

MAKES ABOUT 3 CUPS

1½ cups fresh organic blueberries, frozen

½ cup vanilla organic whole-milk yogurt

1 cup (8 ounces) unfiltered pasteurized organic apple juice

Combine all ingredients in a blender and process until smooth. Strain through a mesh strainer to remove any bits of peel, for the smoothest texture.

TIP

True blue. I was corrected by two-and-a-half-year-old Sam that this shake looked more purple than blue, so it should be called Purpleberry.

NUTRITION FACTS

Serving Size: 1 cup (201g)

Calories   110
Calories from Fat   10
Total Fat   1g
Saturated Fat   0g
Cholesterol   0mg
Sodium   30mg
Total Carbohydrate   25g
Dietary Fiber   2g
Sugars   21g
Protein   2g

the
petit
appetit
COOKBOOK
♥

Potato-Carrot Mash

This is an improvement on the standard mashed potato recipe and easy to make anytime. The great thing is you can make this recipe with leftover baked potatoes or leftover carrot puree for baby. If you have both, simply stir together and continue with recipe. Russet potatoes work best in this recipe as they have a high starch content and will become fluffy.

MAKES 4 SERVINGS

3 medium organic baking potatoes, peeled and cut into chunks
   (about 3 cups)

4 medium organic carrots, peeled and cut into chunks
   (about 2 cups)

½ teaspoon sea salt

¼ cup plain organic whole-milk yogurt

2 tablespoons unsalted butter

1½ teaspoons sweet and hot mustard

Sea salt and white pepper, to taste

Put carrots and potatoes in a large stockpot, cover with cold water, and sprinkle with salt. Bring to a boil over medium-high heat, and boil until tender, about 10 minutes. Transfer potatoes and carrots to a food processor and puree. Stir in yogurt, butter, and mustard. Season with salt and pepper.

TIP

Colored mashed potatoes. There are many colors and healthy mashed potato variations that can be created by adding vegetables. How about asparagus for a green potato puree for St Patrick's Day? Or maybe beets for red potato puree for Valentine's Day? Or make both, green and red for the Christmas table.

EGG FREE

GLUTEN FREE

WHEAT FREE

VEGETARIAN

SUGAR FREE

NUTRITION FACTS

Serving Size: 6 oz (165g)

Calories   160
Calories from Fat   60
Total Fat   6g
Saturated Fat   4g
Cholesterol   15mg
Sodium   410mg
Total Carbohydrate   24g
Dietary Fiber   5g
Sugars   11g
Protein   3g

The
Independents:
Nine to Twelve
Months

♥

Fruity Gelatin

This is a great way for your children to enjoy a cold, wiggly dessert without the added sugars and preservatives of the boxed versions. Real fruit gives more flavor and texture than the processed version.

MAKES 10 TO 12 SERVINGS

1 envelope gelatin
¼ cup hot water
1 cup Apple Puree (page 59), or organic unsweetened applesauce

In a medium bowl, dissolve gelatin in hot water, stirring continuously. Add puree and stir with a rubber spatula to combine. Pour mixture into an 8-inch square or round shallow glass dish, and chill in the refrigerator until firm, about 2 hours.

TIP
Under the weather? This recipe is a cool way to get some fruit and liquids into a sick child. Any of baby's fruit purees from Chapter 7 can be used to create this treat.

NUTRITION FACTS

Serving Size: ⅟₁₀ of recipe
(28g)

Calories 15
Calories from Fat 0
Total Fat 0g
Saturated Fat 0g
Cholesterol 0mg
Sodium 0mg
Total Carbohydrate 2g
Dietary Fiber 0g
Sugars 2g
Protein 1g

the
petit
appetit
COOKBOOK
♥

Edamame Puree

Some call edamame, or vegetable soy beans, the super or wonder food because it is almost the only vegetable that contains all nine essential amino acids. This makes edamame a complete protein source, similar to meat or eggs, which are especially important to vegetarian and vegan babies. My son loves his puree blended with plain yogurt.

MAKES 12 SERVINGS

1 cup fresh or frozen organic green soybeans (edamame), shelled
½ cup purified water

Place fresh soybeans in a steamer basket in a pot filled with about 2 inches of lightly boiling water. Do not let water touch soybeans. Steam fresh soybeans for about 20 minutes. Follow package directions for cooking frozen soybeans.

Puree soybeans in a food processor fitted with a steel blade. Slowly add liquid and continue to process to a smooth paste, about 1 minute. Scrape down sides of bowl midway through processing. Add more water to achieve desired consistency.

NUTRITION FACTS

Serving Size: 2 tablespoons (30g)

Calories 25
Calories from Fat 5
Total Fat 0.5g
Saturated Fat 0g
Cholesterol 0mg
Sodium 0mg
Total Carbohydrate 3g
Dietary Fiber 2g
Sugars 0g
Protein 1g

The
Independents:
Nine to Twelve
Months

♥

Popeye Puree

Today's children probably don't even know Popeye, but most adults remember him fondly chugging those cans of spinach. No wonder everyone thinks spinach is wet, gray, and tasteless. Here's the real deal—very sweet and packed with vitamins.

MAKES 12 TO 14 (1-OUNCE) SERVINGS

1 bunch organic spinach, or 1 (10-ounce) bag frozen organic spinach

Separate leaves and trim from stalks. To clean spinach of all the sand and grit, fill a sink or large basin with lukewarm water. Plunge leaves into sink and swish under water. The silt and sand will sink to the bottom, leaving you with clean leaves.

Steamer Method: Place spinach leaves in a steamer basket set in a pot filled with about 1 to 2 inches of lightly boiling water. Do not let water touch spinach. Cover tightly for best nutrient retention and steam for 2 to 3 minutes, or until spinach is wilted and bright green. Rinse spinach in cold water to stop cooking.

Puree spinach in a food processor. Add 1 or 2 tablespoons of cooking liquid to make the puree smoother and adjust consistency.

Microwave Method: Place spinach in a microwave-safe dish. Add 2 tablespoons water and cover tightly, allowing a corner to vent. Microwave on high for 1 minute and stir spinach. Re-cover and cook for 1 minute, or until wilted and bright. Cool spinach and proceed with directions above.

TIP

Freeze please! If you're worried about the dirt in fresh spinach and don't want to spend time washing it, you can buy organic spinach frozen and ready to use. It will still have much of the same flavor and nutrients. You will not need to add any liquid to process it because of the water from freezing.

NUTRITION FACTS

Serving Size: 1 ounce (28g)

Calories 10
Calories from Fat 0
Total Fat 0g
Saturated Fat 0g
Cholesterol 0mg
Sodium 25mg
Total Carbohydrate 1g
Dietary Fiber 1g
Sugars 0g
Protein 1g

the
petit
appetit
COOKBOOK
♥

Out of the Garden Pancakes

Children who "don't eat vegetables" will eat these pancakes. They are a filling entrée, a hearty snack, or a side dish for grilled meats.

MAKES ABOUT 10 (4-INCH) PANCAKES

1 cup organic broccoli or broccoli florets

12 organic asparagus spears

1 cup (6 ounces) sliced organic brown mushrooms

¼ cup chopped organic onion

1 large garlic clove, minced

¼ cup expeller pressed canola oil

⅔ cup organic whole wheat flour

1 tablespoon fresh dill weed

⅛ teaspoon sea salt

1 large cage-free, organic egg

¼ cup organic milk

1 cup shredded cheddar cheese (optional)

Place broccoli and asparagus in a steamer basket set in a pot filled with about 1 to 2 inches of lightly boiling water. Do not let water touch vegetables. Cover and steam vegetables for 4 to 5 minutes, or until tender.

Put broccoli, asparagus, mushrooms, onion, and garlic in a food processor and pulse on and off to chop, or chop by hand. Be careful not to puree. Transfer chopped ingredients into a large bowl and stir in oil, flour, dill, and salt. Add the egg and milk and mix thoroughly with a wooden spoon.

Heat a large nonstick skillet over medium heat and coat with cooking spray. Drop batter by ¼ cups into the skillet and cook until firm on bottom, about 2 minutes. Turn the pancakes with a spatula and sprinkle cooked side with cheddar cheese, if desired. Cook remaining sides until golden, about 1 minute.

NUTRITION FACTS

Serving Size: 1 pancake (85g)

Calories 150
Calories from Fat 90
Total Fat 10g
Saturated Fat 3g
Cholesterol 35mg
Sodium 115mg
Total Carbohydrate 9g
Dietary Fiber 2g
Sugars 1g
Protein 6g

The Independents: Nine to Twelve Months

♥

TIP

Adult treats. This recipe can become an adult hors d'oeuvres by dropping batter by tablespoonfuls for bite-size treats. Top these pancakes with a spoonful of baby's leftover Apple Puree (page 59) or a dollop of sour cream or crème fraîche.

Nectarine Butter

Fruit butters are great to have on hand for surprising your children by transforming the ordinary into something special. They are delicious spread on breakfast and snack foods such as toast, waffles, pancakes, and breads. Fruit butters can also be a simple dessert over angel food cake or vanilla ice cream.

MAKES ABOUT 15 SERVINGS

2 medium organic nectarines, cut into chunks (about 1½ cups)
½ cup pasteurized unfiltered organic apple juice
½ cup water
½ teaspoon ground cinnamon
¼ teaspoon vanilla extract

Place all ingredients in a small saucepan and simmer over medium heat for about 6 to 8 minutes, or until nectarines are very soft. Drain and reserve liquid. Transfer fruit to a processor or blender and puree.

Press puree through sieve or mesh strainer, and discard fruit pulp. Adjust the texture and consistency to your liking, by adding juice.

TIP
Another butter? Fruit butters can be made with just about any fruit. Hard fruits such as apples and pears will take longer to cook, while softer fruit choices such as berries, papayas, or mangoes will cook in just a few minutes.

NUTRITION FACTS
Serving Size: 2 tablespoons (30g)

Calories 20
Calories from Fat 0
Total Fat 0g
Saturated Fat 0g
Cholesterol 0mg
Sodium 0mg
Total Carbohydrate 4g
Dietary Fiber 0g
Sugars 2g
Protein 0g

The Independents: Nine to Twelve Months

♥

Dilly Ricotta Dip

Ricotta is a favorite among the little ones because of its mild flavor and creamy texture. It is also easily digestible for little tummies. Children love this quick dip for dunking steamed vegetables or crackers. It can also be an unexpected spread for wraps and sandwiches.

MAKES 4 SERVINGS

⅓ cup whole-milk ricotta cheese

1 tablespoon minced fresh dill

1 teaspoon minced fresh mint

2 tablespoons freshly squeezed lemon juice

Combine all ingredients in a small bowl and stir until creamy.

NOTE

Ricotta for the royals? The cheese originated in the countryside around Rome. It was traditionally served to important guests and royalty at celebrations and religious ceremonies. Certainly your little royal deserves such a cheese.

the
petit
appetit
COOKBOOK
♥

Couscous Pudding

Here's a variation of rice pudding using couscous instead of rice. The smaller grain makes this pudding very creamy and smooth. For those who want their pudding sweeter, sprinkle with additional brown sugar or make with vanilla yogurt instead of plain.

MAKES 5 SERVINGS

½ cup organic couscous

1 cup organic whole milk

2 tablespoons organic brown sugar

¼ cup organic golden raisins

1 cup plain organic whole milk yogurt

¼ teaspoon vanilla extract

¼ teaspoon ground cinnamon

In a medium saucepan, heat milk over medium heat just to boiling point. Be careful not to burn. Remove pan from heat and stir in remaining ingredients to combine. Cover and let sit for 20 minutes, or until the couscous absorbs milk and the texture is creamy.

Serve warm or cover and refrigerate until ready to serve. You may need to add more yogurt when reheating if pudding becomes dry.

NOTE

Comfort food. My dad fondly remembers his mother's rice pudding that she made when he was a child. Luckily this recipe passed Dad's taste test and reminded him of hers.

NUTRITION FACTS

Serving Size: ½ cup (126g)

Calories 160
Calories from Fat 15
Total Fat 2g
Saturated Fat 1g
Cholesterol 5mg
Sodium 60mg
Total Carbohydrate 31g
Dietary Fiber 1g
Sugars 13g
Protein 6g

The
Independents:
Nine to Twelve
Months

♥

Cheese Please! Sauce

Some kids won't eat their veggies without a little encouragement. Here's a simple, creamy sauce to help out. This versatile sauce is also good on chicken, fish, and pasta.

MAKES 7 SERVINGS (ABOUT 1½ CUPS TOTAL)

1 tablespoon unsalted butter

2 tablespoons unbleached all-purpose flour

1¼ cups organic whole milk

½ cup grated sharp cheddar cheese

⅛ teaspoon freshly grated nutmeg

In a small saucepan, melt butter over medium-low heat. Add the flour and cook, stirring, until mixture combines to create a thick paste, about 1 minute. Whisk in the milk, a little at a time. Whisk continuously until sauce bubbles and becomes creamy and thick, 5 to 7 minutes. Remove pan from heat and stir in cheese and nutmeg.

TIP

Say cheese. Choose whichever cheese you and your family likes for this recipe. Good melting and tasting options include white cheddar, mozzarella, Gruyère, and Swiss.

NUTRITION FACTS

Serving Size: ¼ cup (56g)

Calories 80
Calories from Fat 45
Total Fat 5g
Saturated Fat 3g
Cholesterol 15mg
Sodium 70mg
Total Carbohydrate 4g
Dietary Fiber 0g
Sugars 0g
Protein 4g

the
petit
appetit
COOKBOOK
♥

Blueberry Syrup

Blueberries are full of vitamins and antioxidants. Besides being good for you, they taste great. This syrup makes everyday pancakes and waffles special. Blueberry syrup also makes a tasty topping for angel food cake.

MAKES 12 SERVINGS

1 pint organic blueberries
¼ cup fresh organic orange juice
1 tablespoon maple syrup

In a small saucepan, combine ingredients and cook over medium-low heat until blueberries pop and sauce thickens into a syrup consistency, about 10 minutes.

NUTRITION FACTS

Serving Size: 2 tablespoons
(31g)

Calories   20
Calories from Fat   0
Total Fat   0g
Saturated Fat   0g
Cholesterol   0mg
Sodium   0mg
Total Carbohydrate   5g
Dietary Fiber   less than 1g
Sugars   4g
Protein   0g

The
Independents:
Nine to Twelve
Months

♥

Anytime Oatmeal

This is a simple oatmeal recipe that you can make once and be prepared to serve your child a hot breakfast for almost a week. This is much tastier, healthier, and less expensive than the prepackaged, flavored oatmeal envelopes.

MAKES 6 (½ CUP) SERVINGS

2 cups quick-cooking organic oats

⅔ cup dry milk

⅓ cup dried organic currants or raisins (optional)

¼ cup toasted organic wheat germ

1 tablespoon organic brown sugar

1 tablespoon ground cinnamon

In a large mixing bowl, combine all ingredients. Mix well with a fork. Transfer to an airtight container.

When ready to eat, measure ½ cup of the mixture into bowl. Add ½ cup boiling water; cover and let sit for 1 minute, and then stir. Top with fresh fruit.

TIP
Creating convenience. This oatmeal mix can be stored in an airtight container for up to two weeks. Stock your pantry with these easy-to-store dry ingredients and you can make oatmeal, as well as lots of other favorites, anytime.

NUTRITION FACTS

Serving Size: ½ cup prepared (168g) (using dry skim milk powder)

Calories 180
Calories from Fat 20
Total Fat 2.5g
Saturated Fat 0g
Cholesterol 0mg
Sodium 50mg
Total Carbohydrate 34g
Dietary Fiber 4g
Sugars 7g
Protein 8g

the
petit
appetit
COOKBOOK
♥

Babes for Brussels

Give these a chance. They are not the old-fashioned overcooked, bitter-tasting sprouts you remember as a child. These are tender with a sweet and savory flavor. Choose small, firm, compact heads with tight-fitting leaves that are bright green in color for the freshest taste.

MAKES 10 SERVINGS

10 ounces organic Brussels sprouts (about 3½ cups)
2 tablespoons extra-virgin olive oil
½ teaspoon black pepper
½ teaspoon sea salt

Preheat oven to 425°F. Line a baking sheet with foil. Trim bottoms of Brussels sprouts, but keep leaves intact. Cut each sprout in half lengthwise. Place sprouts in a plastic bag with oil and toss to coat. Place sprouts on baking sheet, season with salt and pepper, and bake for 15 minutes, turning halfway through. Bake until outside leaves begin to brown and crisp and inside is fork tender.

TIP
Little heads for little hands. These make a great snack for toddler hands. Some even like to peel and eat them leaf by leaf.

NUTRITION FACTS
Serving Size: 1 ounce (28g)

Calories   35
Calories from Fat   25
Total Fat   3g
Saturated Fat   0g
Cholesterol   0mg
Sodium   120mg
Total Carbohydrate   2g
Dietary Fiber less than   1 g
Sugars   0g
Protein   1g

The
Independents:
Nine to Twelve
Months

♥

Baked Bananafanas

This is an easy treat for all ages. Babies and toddlers can eat the bananas alone, topped with yogurt, or cut on top of waffles and pancakes. For a great adult dessert, top bananas with ice cream and a drizzle of rum.

MAKES 4 SERVINGS

2 large, ripe organic bananas
1 tablespoon organic orange juice
1 teaspoon maple syrup
Cinnamon, for sprinkling

Preheat oven to 350°F. Lightly grease a glass baking dish. Cut bananas in half crosswise and lengthwise, so there will be 8 pieces. In a small bowl, combine orange juice and syrup. Place bananas in greased dish and spoon syrup mixture over each banana. Sprinkle with cinnamon. Bake bananas for 15 minutes, or until soft and golden.

TIP
Ripe to it! This is a great way to save and enjoy those brown-speckled, overripe bananas.

Petite Bulgur Bowl

Bulgur is a cracked wheat. Also called ALA, it is a staple in Middle Eastern cooking, used in salads, and mixed with meats and vegetables. This is a great hot cereal to make once and have on hand for the entire week. Individual servings can be ready any day in just one minute.

MAKES 4 CUPS

½ cup organic bulgur
½ cup golden organic raisins
1 cup boiling water
Honey (optional), for serving

Put bulgur and raisins in a glass bowl. Add boiling water. Cover tightly and let sit until water has been absorbed, about 1 hour. This can be refrigerated for up to 4 days.

To reheat, place ½ cup of the bulgur mixture in a small bowl and drizzle with ¼ teaspoon honey, if desired. Cover and vent corner. Heat in microwave on High for 1 minute. Serve with fresh fruit and yogurt.

TIP
Bulgur for baby. Remember: if this is your baby's first taste of wheat, introduce by feeding for five consecutive days and watch for any allergic reaction.

NUTRITION FACTS

Serving Size: 1 cup (47g)

Calories   60
Calories from Fat   0
Total Fat   0g
Saturated Fat   0g
Cholesterol   0mg
Sodium   0mg
Total Carbohydrate   14g
Dietary Fiber   2g
Sugars   5g
Protein   1g

The
Independents:
Nine to Twelve
Months

♥

NUTRITION FACTS

Serving Size: 1 baton (9g)

Calories 35
Calories from Fat 10
Total Fat 1g
Saturated Fat 0.5g
Cholesterol 5mg
Sodium 5mg
Total Carbohydrate 5g
Dietary Fiber 0g
Sugars 2g
Protein 1g

Cereal Batons

When I started Petit Appetit I sold these cookies through local retail outlets, and they became favorite giveaways at children's parties and events. No wonder. This cookie is both sweet and crunchy, which children can't resist. Your child won't know your secret crunchy ingredient is wheat germ. Wheat germ can be purchased raw or pretoasted.

MAKES 90 (2½-INCH) BATONS

½ cup unsalted butter

1 cup raw organic sugar

2 cage-free, organic eggs

1 teaspoon vanilla extract

2½ cups organic whole-wheat flour

¼ teaspoon baking soda

½ cup toasted organic wheat germ

Heat oven to 400°F. Place butter in microwave on High for 20 seconds to soften. Blend together first six ingredients, plus ¼ cup of the wheat germ. Work dough with hands to combine. Roll 2 tablespoons of dough into small balls and then stick/baton shapes. Spread remaining ¼ cup wheat germ on waxed paper. Roll batons in wheat germ to coat. Place on greased or parchment lined baking sheets and bake for 6 to 8 minutes, or until light brown.

He never takes to food like that. Cole is a very picky eater, even when it comes to sweets, and he's going after these cookies.

ONE-YEAR-OLD COLE'S mom

Cottage Noodles

Here's an easy and more nutritious alternative to standard buttered noodles. The cottage cheese provides protein and calcium and the cinnamon gives some sweetness. If making this for someone less than one year old, you may want to use egg-free noodles.

MAKES 2 SERVINGS

8 ounces uncooked wide noodles
½ cup small-curd cottage cheese
½ teaspoon ground cinnamon

Cook noodles according to manufacturer's instructions. Drain and toss hot noodles with cottage cheese and cinnamon.

Anya likes noodles with raisins. She won't eat plain raisins or plain noodles, but she will eat them all day when they're together.

TWO-YEAR-OLD ANYA'S mom

The
Independents:
Nine to Twelve
Months

♥

Fruity Puree Cookies

This is Petit Appetit's most popular cookie. Now you can make these treats at home. Make extra Apple Puree (page 59) or get baby to share, so you can make these anytime. Pear puree works well, too.

MAKES ABOUT 100 COOKIES

¾ cup organic brown sugar

¾ cup expeller pressed canola oil

1 cup Apple Puree (page 59) or unsweetened organic applesauce

½ teaspoon salt

1 teaspoon vanilla extract

½ cup organic oat bran

½ cup organic toasted wheat germ

1½ cup organic whole wheat flour

½ cup organic soy flour

Heat oven to 350°F. Combine sugar and oil in a medium bowl until smooth. Add remaining ingredients, one at a time, mixing after each addition. Refrigerate dough for 30 minutes. Roll 1 tablespoon-pieces of dough into balls and place on greased or parchment-lined baking sheets. Flatten cookies with a fork that has been dipped in flour. Bake for 12 to 14 minutes, or until golden brown underneath. Remove cookies with a spatula and let cool on wire racks.

TIP
Wheat germ comes in raw and toasted versions. You can find them both in the bulk food section of specialty grocery stores or in glass containers in the cereal aisle. Toasted germ has a bit more crunch and a nuttier flavor. Either can be used here.

NUTRITION FACTS

Serving Size: 3 cookies
(30g)

Calories 110
Calories from Fat 60
Total Fat 6g
Saturated Fat 0.5g
Cholesterol 0mg
Sodium 40mg
Total Carbohydrate 13g
Dietary Fiber 2g
Sugars 6g
Protein 3 g

the
petit
appetit
COOKBOOK
♥

Mac Cheese with Vegetables

Macaroni and cheese is a favorite for any age. This is much tastier and healthier than the box version, and only takes a few more minutes to make. Make this with assorted vegetables or a single vegetable. Broccoli and cauliflower pieces are a convenient choice because the cooking time is the same for the pasta. You can also dress up this everyday favorite with a variety of pasta shapes. You may choose to omit the Parmesan and extra time in the oven, but I wouldn't.

MAKES 4 TO 6 SERVINGS

8 ounces elbow macaroni (see note below)

1½ cups organic broccoli and/or cauliflower florets, cut into equal-size pieces

1 cup organic whole milk

3 cups (¾ pound) shredded sharp white cheddar cheese

Salt, to taste

¼ teaspoon freshly ground black pepper

3 tablespoons freshly grated Parmesan cheese

Preheat oven to 350°F. Bring a pot of water to a boil over high heat. Turn heat to medium and add macaroni and vegetables. Simmer until macaroni is tender and vegetables are cooked, but not mushy, 7 to 10 minutes. Drain water from pasta and vegetables and return to cooking pot.

In a small saucepan, heat milk over low heat until hot. Add cheddar cheese and hot milk to vegetables and macaroni and toss. Season with salt and pepper. Pour mixture into an 8-inch square glass or ceramic baking dish. Sprinkle Parmesan cheese over top and bake for 15 minutes, or until bubbling. Allow to sit for 5 to 10 minutes before serving.

NOTE
For those under one year, use egg-free noodles.

NUTRITION FACTS

Serving Size: 1 cup (252g)

Calories 490
Calories from Fat 240
Total Fat 27g
Saturated Fat 18g
Cholesterol 80mg
Sodium 620mg
Total Carbohydrate 35g
Dietary Fiber 2g
Sugars 1g
Protein 23g

The
Independents:
Nine to Twelve
Months

♥

Wheat-Free Fruity Puree Cookies

This is a variation on the popular Fruity Puree Cookies (page 128) for those who cannot eat wheat. The brown rice flour makes these cookies lighter in color and flavor than the original.

MAKES ABOUT 100 PIECES

¾ cup organic brown sugar

¾ cup expeller pressed canola oil

1 cup Apple Puree (page 59), or unsweetened organic applesauce

½ teaspoon salt

1 teaspoon vanilla extract

1 cup organic oat bran

2 cups organic brown rice flour

Heat oven to 350°F. Mix sugar and oil in a small bowl until smooth. Add remaining ingredients, one at a time, mixing after each addition. Roll 1-tablespoon-size pieces of dough into balls and place on greased or parchment-lined baking sheets. Flatten cookies with fork, dipped in flour. Bake 12 to 14 minutes, or until golden underneath. Cookies will be light colored on top. Remove cookies from sheet with a spatula and place on wire racks to cool.

When I gave Emma these cookies, she kept saying, "Mo . . . mo," which is about the best testimonial you can get. She only says about six words, "Mo," or more, being one of them.

EIGHTEEN-MONTH-OLD ELLA'S dad

NUTRITION FACTS

Serving Size: 3 cookies (30g)

Calories   110
Calories from Fat   50
Total Fat   6g
Saturated Fat   0g
Cholesterol   0mg
Sodium   40mg
Total Carbohydrate   15g
Dietary Fiber   less than 1 g
Sugars   6g
Protein   1g

The
Independents:
Nine to Twelve
Months

♥

Happy Hummus

Hummus makes a great dip with vegetables for toddlers, as well as quick hors d'oeuvres for parents. Hummus is also an alternative spread for sandwiches, bagels, and toast. At ten months, this was my son's favorite food, especially spread on small pieces of whole-wheat toast.

MAKES 2⅓ CUPS

2 cups cooked or canned organic chickpeas (garbanzo beans)

⅓ cup tahini sauce (sesame seed paste)

1 large clove garlic, minced

Juice of 1 lemon

2 tablespoon extra-virgin olive oil

½ teaspoon ground cumin

If using canned chickpeas, drain and rinse thoroughly until water is clear. Process chickpeas, tahini, garlic, lemon juice, 1 tablespoon of the oil, and cumin in a food processor or blender until pureed. Scrape down sides of bowl and add remaining 1 tablespoon oil. Process for 20 to 30 seconds, or until pastelike. If you want a smoother consistency, add more oil or lemon juice and continue to process.

TIP

You say garbanzo, I say chickpea. Some people call these beans chickpeas while others refer to them as garbanzo beans. Either way they are a great source of protein for the whole family.

NUTRITION FACTS

Serving Size: 2 tablespoons (30g)

Calories 60
Calories from Fat 30
Total Fat 3g
Saturated Fat 0g
Cholesterol 0mg
Sodium 70mg
Total Carbohydrate 6g
Dietary Fiber 1g
Sugars 0g
Protein 2g

the
petit
appetit
COOKBOOK

♥

Baked Sweet-Potato Chips

Unlike commercially processed potato chips, these chips require very little oil and no frying. That makes them a good choice for all ages. You can bake them plain or for variety, sprinkle with herbs and spices. You can sprinkle them with salt and pepper, or cumin for a savory flavor. And try topping with nutmeg or cinnamon for a sweet option. They are also good dipped in yogurt or salsa (page 177).

MAKES 18 CHIPS

1 large (8- to 9-ounce) organic sweet potato, thinly sliced
2 tablespoons olive oil
Sea salt, pepper, or other dried herbs, to taste (optional)

Preheat oven to 425°F. Line a large baking sheet with foil and grease. Thinly slice potato into ⅛-inch thick slices, using a mandolin or steady, sharp knife. Put potato slices into a plastic self-sealing bag. Drizzle potatoes with oil. Move plastic bag around potatoes to coat all sides.

Place individual potato slices in a single layer on prepared baking sheet. Sprinkle with salt, if desired. Bake for 15 to 20 minutes, depending on how crisp you like them. Remove potato slices and place on a wire rack to cool.

TIP
Careful cutting. Choose a smooth and even sweet potato. Crooked potatoes make for difficult and dangerous cutting.

NUTRITION FACTS

Serving Size: 2 chips (28g)

Calories 60
Calories from Fat 25
Total Fat 3g
Saturated Fat 0g
Cholesterol 0mg
Sodium 0mg
Total Carbohydrate 7g
Dietary Fiber 1g
Sugars 5g
Protein 1g

The
Independents:
Nine to Twelve
Months

♥

Chapter 10 ♥

The Movers: Twelve to Twenty-four Months

Introduction Map		
(Can eat all Independents' food, plus the following)		
FOODS APPROPRIATE	REASON	CONSISTENCY/TEXTURE
Liquids: whole cow's milk, water, juice	Can now give whole cow's milk. A valuable source of vitamins, other nutrients, and fats needed for development.	
Table foods, including potential allergens avoided previously, such as tomatoes, corn, and strawberries	Now have enzymes to digest foods previously avoided	Cut various foods into small enough pieces to allow self-feeding, yet avoid choking. Child will become better at using utensils and self-feeding.

HOW MUCH?

The American Academy of Pediatrics recommends building good eating habits with children eating five to six times per day. Three meals and two to three snacks is a good way to meet toddlers' energy needs. Children should be drinking sixteen to twenty-four ounces of cow's milk.

READY?

They are moving and toddling about and need fuel to sustain their activity level. As far as eating goes, they are all over the board. Snacks continue to be where they get much of their calories. Most like to dip foods and may come up with some interesting combinations. Samantha (age fifteen months) dipped grapes into ketchup. Keiley (age twenty-two months) dipped everything in mustard and politely asked throughout her dinner, "mo' musta pease." At the end of this stage many children become picky or choosy eaters and may want the same food at every meal, eat only certain colored foods (one client went through a "white only" stage), no longer want food in pieces but whole, and say "no" to everything being offered. Often parents give in and become short-order cooks, making special meals on demand.

SET?

If your child's diet has been varied up until now, their "choosey" stage may not be as difficult. If they once ate twenty different foods and now will only eat ten, you'll have an easier time than if they only liked ten to begin with. Offer one new food with some familiar favorites and let them choose. Be consistent with your parenting in the kitchen at this stage. If your child knows you will make a special meal for them, they will hold out and wait for you to do the same at the next meal. It's up to you to continue to challenge them with new tastes and textures and instill good eating habits.

> *Don't be surprised if your child tosses food on the floor. At age one, my son pointed a finger at everything he wanted. If I gave him food he didn't want, he threw it on the floor in defiance.*
>
> SIXTEEN-MONTH-OLD ERIC'S mom

GO!

Now you have the green light to feed them just about any foods, including those mentioned in Chapter 6. When you begin serving cow's milk, it is recommended for children to drink whole milk until age two. Reduced-fat or no-fat milk doesn't have enough fat and calories for a growing baby. Do not switch to lower fat milk and milk products such as yogurt and cheese until the baby's doctor recommends this change.

Be creative and keep their interest. This does not mean every meal must be fancy and come with a toy surprise, but keep in mind that children are very visual and a fun-shaped pancake on a Sunday morning may make their day. This chapter has lots of creative ideas for snacks, family meals, and travel foods. Variety is the spice of life. Offer them everything, even spicy and ethnic foods. Emma (eighteen months) kept grabbing at her dad's curry chicken at an Indian restaurant. Finally he let her try it, and she loved it!

Children notice everything that you and the rest of the family are doing and this includes what you are eating. Be a good role model and create fast and convenient meals at home, rather than going through a drive-thru or heading to the grocery freezer section. Children also watch other children. If your child sees a friend enjoying broccoli, they just might eat some, too.

> We never prepare special meals for them. Everyone eats the same thing at mealtime and the kids are required to at least try new items. Then if they don't like it, it's okay not to eat it. Most often they like it. Also, if my husband or I don't like a food, we don't let our kids know it. That way we are not prejudicing their tastes.
>
> YVONNE, mother of three (ages three, five, and eight)

CAUTION: SLOW DOWN

This may not be an easy task when your toddler would rather be moving than sitting still. However if they are eating while moving, toddling, strolling, riding in a car, playing, or doing anything outside of being seated in their feeding chair, the risk of choking increases tremendously. Avoid chewy, sticky foods and ones that are too hard, which can become choking hazards. See Chapter 5, about food safety and foods to avoid.

The Movers: Recipes

Salmon with Rice

Salmon is rich in healthy omega-3 oils and protein, important parts of your family's diet. This dish is an easy one-pot supper for Mom, Dad, and Baby. This dish can be multiplied for a large family, or a small one with a big appetite; figure on 4 ounces of fish per adult.

MAKES 2 SERVINGS

1¾ cups organic vegetable broth

1 (8-ounce) wild salmon fillet, skinned

¾ cup uncooked short-grain organic brown rice

1 large shallot, chopped (about 2 tablespoons)

1 tablespoon unsalted butter

2 tablespoons chopped fresh parsley

1 tablespoon freshly squeezed lemon juice

1 cup water

In a large saucepan, bring broth to a boil. Add salmon to broth, cover, and poach in simmering liquid for about 5 minutes, or until cooked throughout. Transfer salmon with a slotted spoon to a plate and cover with foil. Return broth to a boil and stir in remaining ingredients. Cover and simmer over medium heat until rice is cooked and tender, 30 to 35 minutes. Break salmon into pieces and add to rice mixture. Cook over medium heat until salmon is heated through, 1 to 2 minutes.

NUTRITION FACTS

Serving Size: 4 ounces fish
plus rice (386g)

Calories 560
Calories from Fat 150
Total Fat 16g
Saturated Fat 6g
Sodium 660mg
Total Carbohydrate 64g
Dietary Fiber 4g
Sugars 5g
Protein 38g

The Movers:
Twelve to
Twenty-four
Months

♥

Vegetarian Chili

This chili is packed with vitamins, protein, fiber, and flavor and fits with almost everyone's diet restrictions. Although meatless, this recipe is a hearty meal perfect for a chilly afternoon or evening.

MAKES 10 (1-CUP) SERVINGS

1 tablespoon extra-virgin olive oil

1 medium organic onion, diced (about 1½ cups)

2 cloves garlic, minced

1 small organic zucchini, diced (about 1 cup)

1 medium organic summer squash, diced (about 1 cup)

1 medium organic red bell pepper, diced (about 1 cup)

1 medium organic green bell pepper, diced (about 1 cup)

½ teaspoon black pepper

½ teaspoon salt

1 tablespoon chili powder

1 teaspoon ground cumin

1 (16-ounce) can organic pinto beans, drained and rinsed

1 (16-ounce) can organic black beans, drained and rinsed

1 (16-ounce) can organic red kidney beans, drained and rinsed

1 (26-ounce) container cut Pomi tomatoes

1 tablespoon mild molasses

Heat oil in a large stockpot over medium heat. Add onion and garlic and cook until soft, about 2 minutes. Add squashes and bell peppers and cook until soft, about 5 minutes. Stir in remaining ingredients and bring to a boil. Reduce heat, cover, and simmer until vegetables are tender, 20 to 25 minutes, stirring occasionally.

NUTRITION FACTS

Serving Size: 1 cup (325g)

Calories 190
Calories from Fat 25
Total Fat 2.5g
Saturated Fat 0g
Cholesterol 0mg
Sodium 760mg
Total Carbohydrate 36g
Dietary Fiber 11g
Sugars 6g
Protein 10g

the
petit
appetit
COOKBOOK
♥

Patriot Parfait

Celebrate Independence Day with a red, white, and blue treat. Kids (and adults) love to see this tasty flag in clear glass bowls. Cheers to the red, white, and blue!

MAKES 6 SERVINGS

1 pint organic strawberries
1 pint organic blueberries
1 quart plain or vanilla organic whole milk yogurt
1 recipe Blueberry Syrup (page 121)

Layer the fruit and yogurt starting with the strawberries on bottom, and ending with the blueberries on top. Drizzle syrup over blueberries.

The Movers:
Twelve to
Twenty-four
Months

♥

Oven-Baked Fries

We all know children love french fries. Unfortunately those in fast food restaurants and freezer sections have little nutritional value and have lots of partially hydrogenated oils, preservatives, and sodium. Be patient while baking, so the fries get crisp with minimal handling. Yes, these may take longer than a trip to the drive-through, but they're well worth it.

MAKES ABOUT 36 (½ X 5-INCH) FRIES; 6 SERVINGS

2 large (about ¾ pound) organic russet potatoes
2 tablespoons extra-virgin olive oil
Sea salt and black pepper, to taste (optional)

Preheat oven to 350°F. Cut potatoes into desired sticks using a mandolin, or cut potatoes carefully by hand lengthwise into 4 large slices. Cut each slice lengthwise into sticks of desired thickness. Place fries in a plastic self-sealing bag and add oil. Move fries around inside bag, to coat all sides. Arrange fries on parchment-lined baking sheets and bake for 30 minutes. Sprinkle with salt and pepper, if desired. Turn fries with a spatula and bake for another 30 minutes, or until fries are crisp and golden brown.

TIP
A-peeling to your child? I've left the skins on these fries; however, if your child doesn't like the brown appearance, peel the potatoes before cutting.

NUTRITION FACTS

Serving Size: 4 ounces
(118g)

Calories   150
Calories from Fat   45
Total Fat   5g
Saturated Fat   0.5g
Cholesterol   0mg
Sodium   105mg
Total Carbohydrate   24g
Dietary Fiber   3g
Sugars   1g
Protein   3g

the
petit
appetit
COOKBOOK
♥

Oh My Omelet

Everyone agrees eggs can be a safe and healthy part of your child's diet after age one. Omelets are a great way to eat eggs as well as get some vegetables in choosy eaters. Grating the vegetables makes them less likely to be picked out. Omelets also make good use of small amounts of veggies and leftovers.

MAKES 3 SERVINGS

5 cage-free, organic eggs

1 tablespoon milk

1 tablespoon expeller pressed canola oil

¼ cup grated organic bell pepper

¼ cup grated organic broccoli, asparagus, squash, or combination

1 tablespoon unsalted butter

¼ cup diced organic tomato

¼ cup shredded cheddar cheese

1 tablespoon fresh thyme, dill, sage, or oregano, or combination

Whisk together eggs and milk in a medium bowl. Heat oil in a large nonstick skillet over medium heat. Add vegetables, except tomato, and cook until tender, 5 to 6 minutes. Remove vegetables, but keep pan on heat. Melt butter in skillet. Pour eggs into pan. Let cook and just before set, add vegetables, tomato, cheese, and herbs to one side of eggs. Let cook for 1 minute more and using a spatula, fold omelet over vegetables. Cook until eggs are firm, then carefully transfer omelet to a plate with a spatula. Cut into wedges.

TIP

Egg-ceptional snack! Pieces of omelet make great snacks and finger food. Just be sure eggs are cooked firm enough for little fingers to successfully handle. Stuff omelet slices into a pita pocket or roll up in a soft tortilla for an easy, on-the-go treat.

NUTRITION FACTS

Serving Size: ⅓ of omelet (158g)

Calories 250
Calories from Fat 180
Total Fat 20g
Saturated Fat 7g
Cholesterol 375mg
Sodium 180mg
Total Carbohydrate 3g
Dietary Fiber less than 1g
Sugars 2g
Protein 14g

The Movers:
Twelve to
Twenty-four
Months

♥

SUGAR
FREE

Mom's Meat Loaf

Why is it meat loaf and not something sexier like "beefcake?" This version has some unexpected veggies inside for choosey eaters. Serve with Roasted Red Pepper Puree (page 176) or ketchup for dipping. The Potato-Carrot Mash (page 111) is the perfect side dish.

MAKES 10 SERVINGS

¼ cup diced organic red pepper

¼ cup diced organic carrot

¼ cup diced organic onion

2 cage-free, organic eggs, slightly beaten

¼ cup milk

1 tablespoon chopped fresh parsley

1 tablespoon Worcestershire sauce

2 tablespoons freshly grated Parmesan cheese

¼ teaspoon sea salt

¼ teaspoon black pepper

¼ cup dry bread crumbs

2 pounds organic lean ground beef (no more than 10 percent fat)

Preheat oven to 375°F. Line a shallow baking pan with aluminum foil, and grease with cooking oil. In a large bowl, combine all ingredients except beef. Add beef and mix with a rubber spatula or your hands, so everything is evenly distributed. Shape meat mixture into desired shape and place in prepared pan. It is best if meat does not touch sides of pan. Bake meat loaf for 45 to 55 minutes, or until cooked through. Allow meat to rest for 10 minutes.

TIP

Shape it up! A meat loaf can be formed into a traditional square or rectangle shape, but how about a fish or a heart? This recipe also works well in greased muffin pans. This is fun for kids and will make about 24 round beef cakes, and takes less time to cook, 30 to 35 minutes.

NUTRITION FACTS

Serving Size: 4 ounces
(113g)

Calories   170
Calories from Fat   80
Total Fat   9g
Saturated Fat   3.5g
Cholesterol   70mg
Sodium   180mg
Total Carbohydrate   3g
Dietary Fiber   0g
Sugars   1g
Protein   19g

the
petit
appetit
COOKBOOK
♥

Greatest Graham Crackers

Like many children, I consider myself a graham cracker junkie. I got hooked when I was pregnant. Unfortunately I learned in a cooking class taught by Kim Severson, author of *The Trans Fat Solution*, that this favorite snack contained partially hydrogenated oils and thus trans fats. I set out to make my own version for the children— and myself. If you like them crisp, roll them very thin. For cookielike crackers, make them a bit thicker.

MAKES ABOUT 48 CRACKERS

1 cup organic graham or whole-wheat flour

1 cup unbleached all-purpose flour

1 teaspoon baking powder

¼ cup unsalted butter

½ cup honey

¼ cup organic milk, plus 1 tablespoon extra for brushing

Preheat oven to 400°F. Combine flours and baking powder in a medium bowl. Cut in butter until the consistency of cornmeal. Mix in honey; dough will still be lumpy. Mix in milk until a stiff dough comes together.

Roll out dough on a liberally floured surface to ¼-inch thickness. Cut into squares or use cookie cutters to make desired shapes. Prick each cracker with a fork and brush with milk.

Bake crackers on ungreased baking sheets for 12 to 15 minutes, or until golden brown. Remove pan from oven and let crackers cool about 2 minutes. Transfer to a wire rack and let cool completely

TIP

Cut it out. Of course, these can be cut to look like traditional store-bought graham crackers. However if you want something more fun (toddlers can help), use your cookie cutters to create desired shapes. Little hands love hearts, flowers, and stars.

EGG FREE

VEGETARIAN

NUTRITION FACTS

Serving Size: 2 crackers
(24g)

Calories 90
Calories from Fat 20
Total Fat 2g
Saturated Fat 1g
Cholesterol 5mg
Sodium 20mg
Total Carbohydrate 16g
Dietary Fiber less than 1g
Sugars 6g
Protein 2g

The Movers:
Twelve to
Twenty-four
Months

♥

the
petit
appetit
COOKBOOK

♥

Baked Ricotta Cake

These cakes are light with a subtle sweetness. Enjoyed out of the ramekin, this recipe reminds me of a healthier, lighter, and easier version of a crème brûlée dessert.

MAKES 6 SERVINGS

1 cup whole-milk ricotta cheese
2 cage-free, organic egg whites
4 tablespoons honey
2 cups mixed fresh organic berries (optional)

Preheat oven to 350°F. Place the cheese in a bowl and break up with a wooden spoon. Beat egg whites in a small bowl until soft peaks form. Add eggs whites and honey to cheese and mix thoroughly until smooth.

Lightly grease 4 ramekins. Spoon ricotta mixture into ramekins. Bake for 30 to 35 minutes, or until cakes are risen and golden.

Cool, turn out of ramekin, and top with berries, if desired. Or enjoy warm out of the ramekin with berries on the side.

TIP

Ricotta ready! Ricotta is recommended for babies because of the mild flavor and creamy texture. It also has less sodium than cottage cheese, used in similar recipes. Ricotta comes in whole-milk, low-fat, and skim-milk versions.

Baby Bok Choy

Bok choy is an Asian member of the cabbage family that has a mild flavor. It consists of long, thick, white stalks, topped by intensely blue-green leaves. Bok choy is a familiar vegetable in Chinese restaurants, where it appears in wonton soup and many stir-fried dishes. It has a high water content and becomes limp immediately upon cooking. It should be cooked quickly over high temperature so that the leaves become tender and the stalks stay crisp.

MAKES 4 SERVINGS

2 tablespoons extra-virgin olive oil

2 teaspoons minced garlic (2 to 3 cloves)

2 teaspoons grated ginger, (1 inch piece)

1 bunch (8 ounces) organic baby bok choy

¼ cup organic vegetable broth

Heat oil in a stockpot over medium heat. Add garlic and ginger and sauté until aromatic, about 1 minute. Add bok choy and cook for 2 minutes. Pour in broth; cover and cook for 3 to 4 minutes, or until greens are tender and bright green.

TIP

Prep Tip. Take a bunch of bok choy and remove each stalk from the outside in. Each stalk can then be washed individually. Rinse stalks and leaves under running water, and pat dry with paper towels. If stalks are especially dirty, scrub gently with a vegetable brush.

NUTRITION FACTS

Serving Size: 3 oz

Calories 80
Calories from Fat 70
Total Fat 8g
Saturated Fat 1g
Cholesterol 0mg
Sodium 65mg
Total Carbohydrate 2g
Dietary Fiber 0g
Sugars 0g
Protein 1g

The Movers:
Twelve to
Twenty-four
Months

♥

Very Vanilla Shake

This shake has no ice cream, but is surprisingly creamy because of the frozen bananas and milk.

MAKES 3 SERVINGS

1 large organic banana, frozen

1 tablespoon vanilla extract

1 cup ice

1 cup organic milk

1 tablespoon honey

Cut frozen banana into equal-size chunks. Put all ingredients in a blender and process until smooth.

TIP

Warm milk. Not all children like cold food and beverages. Don't be surprised if your little one asks you to heat this up to room temperature.

NUTRITION FACTS

Serving Size: 1 cup (217g)

Calories   110
Calories from Fat   15
Total Fat   2g
Saturated Fat   1g
Cholesterol   5mg
Sodium   40mg
Total Carbohydrate   21g
Dietary Fiber   1g
Sugars   12g
Protein   3g

the
petit
appetit
COOKBOOK
♥

Sweet and Savory Yogurt Dip

This dip is easy and unexpected for Sweet Potato Chips (page 133), kabobs (page 151), or steamed vegetables. A mom in one of my classes revealed to me that cumin was her secret ingredient in many of her family dishes. I can see why, as it lends both a sweet and savory flavor.

MAKES 3 SERVINGS

⅓ cup plain organic whole-milk yogurt

1 teaspoon ground cumin

1 teaspoon ground cinnamon

1 teaspoon organic brown sugar

Combine all ingredients in a small bowl until creamy.

NUTRITION FACTS

Serving Size: 2 tablespoons (30g)

Calories 30
Calories from Fat 5
Total Fat 0.5g
Saturated Fat 0g
Cholesterol 0mg
Sodium 20mg
Total Carbohydrate 4g
Dietary Fiber less than 1g
Sugars 3g
Protein 2g

The Movers:
Twelve to
Twenty-four
Months

♥

Garden Tomato Sauce

This is a hearty and healthy tomato sauce to serve over pasta or vegetables. If you choose not to roast your own tomatoes, you can substitute ready-to-eat Pomi tomatoes. Many people remove the tomato seeds when making sauce; however, I find it's much easier, and more nutritious, to keep them in.

MAKES 8 SERVINGS

1 pound vine-ripened organic tomatoes, or 1 (16-ounce) container Pomi tomatoes

1 tablespoon extra-virgin olive oil

1 medium organic onion, chopped (about 1 cup)

⅓ cup diced organic green bell pepper

1 cup (6 ounces) diced organic mushrooms

2 cloves garlic, minced

2 teaspoons dried oregano

2 teaspoons dried basil

1 bay leaf

½ teaspoon sea salt

½ cup organic vegetable broth

1 tablespoon organic tomato paste

1 teaspoon honey

If using fresh tomatoes, preheat oven to broil. Pierce each tomato with a small knife and place tomatoes in a baking pan. Broil tomatoes until skins split and begin to turn brown, turning halfway through cooking, 15 minutes. Once cool, peel off tomato skins and puree in a food processor. If using Pomi tomatoes, simply puree.

Heat olive oil in a large skillet over medium heat. Add onion and bell pepper and sauté until onion is soft, 5 minutes. Add mushrooms, garlic, herbs, salt, broth, tomato paste, and pureed tomatoes to skillet and stir. Simmer mixture, uncovered, over low heat for 30 minutes. Remove bay leaf. Add honey and cook for another 10 minutes.

TIP

Meaty mushrooms. The mushrooms give this vegetarian sauce a "meaty" texture and flavor. Be careful when storing and handling mushrooms as they bruise and spoil easily. Store in the coldest part of the refrigerator in a paper bag or wrapped in a paper towel. Do not store in a plastic bag as this can make mushrooms slimy.

NUTRITION FACTS

Serving Size: ½ cup (113g)

Calories 50
Calories from Fat 15
Total Fat 2g
Saturated Fat 0g
Cholesterol 0mg
Sodium 190mg
Total Carbohydrate 7g
Dietary Fiber 1g
Sugars 4g
Protein 1g

the
petit
appetit
COOKBOOK
♥

Egg-cellent Pizza

This takes the idea of pizza for breakfast one step further. This recipe was inspired by Rose's Café in San Francisco. There you'll find families with highchairs looking forward to their breakfast pizzas.

MAKES 1 (12- TO 14-INCH) PIZZA; 6 SERVINGS

1 recipe Presto Pizza Dough (page 197)
1 recipe Spinach Pesto sauce (page 269)
4 cage-free, organic eggs
½ cup grated Parmesan cheese

Preheat oven to 425°F. Place dough on an oiled baking sheet or pizza pan and press fingers to spread into desired shape. Partially bake dough for 10 minutes. Remove from oven and top with pesto sauce. Crack eggs onto pizza and sprinkle with cheese. Bake for 10 minutes, or until eggs are cooked and dough is golden and crisp to desired doneness.

VARIATION
Green Eggs and Ham Pizza: For meat eaters, add Canadian bacon or prosciutto, an Italian ham, to this pizza.

NUTRITION FACTS

Serving Size: ⅙ of Pizza
(134g)

Calories 350
Calories from Fat 180
Total Fat 20g
Saturated Fat 5g
Cholesterol 150mg
Sodium 550mg
Total Carbohydrate 29g
Dietary Fiber 5g
Sugars 0g
Protein 15g

The Movers:
Twelve to
Twenty-four
Months

♥

Happy Days Egg and Olive Spread

Many adults think of egg salad and olive spread as comforting foods from their childhood. This recipe combines the best of both. The lemon and yogurt give this spread a new fresh taste and healthy alternative to the standard mayonnaise flavor, which many children do not like.

MAKES 15 (2-TABLESPOON) SERVINGS

2 hard-cooked, cage-free organic eggs
⅓ cup pitted black olives (about 10 whole), chopped
1 tablespoon freshly squeezed lemon juice
1 tablespoon plain organic whole-milk yogurt
Salt and black pepper, to taste

Chop eggs finely using an egg slicer or knife. Mix all ingredients together in a small bowl until combined.

VARIATION
Sandwich bread alternative. Stuff this spread into pita bread with arugula, or roll it up in spinach leaves.

NUTRITION FACTS

Serving Size: 2 tablespoons
(30g)

Calories 25
Calories from Fat   10
Total Fat   1g
Saturated Fat   0g
Cholesterol   25mg
Sodium   45mg
Total Carbohydrate   2g
Dietary Fiber   0g
Sugars   2g
Protein   2g

the
petit
appetit
COOKBOOK

♥

Baked Chicken Bites

Toddlers love chicken they can pick up and dip. Because the chicken is quality white meat, there's no guessing what's in the "nugget." They are a healthy twist to the usual fried strips found in restaurants and freezer aisles.

MAKES 4 SERVINGS

2 skinless, boneless organic chicken breasts

1 tablespoon freshly squeezed lemon juice

1 tablespoon olive oil

1 teaspoon minced garlic

1 tablespoon prepared mustard

1 cup dry bread crumbs

Preheat oven to 375°F. Cut chicken breasts into desired size strips. In a medium glass bowl, combine lemon juice, oil, garlic, and mustard. Add cut chicken to lemon mixture and marinate in the refrigerator for 30 minutes or longer. Spread breadcrumbs on a plate or wax paper. Remove chicken pieces and roll in bread crumbs to coat. Place chicken pieces on lightly oiled or parchment lined baking sheet and bake in the oven for 20 minutes, turning after 10 minutes. Be sure sides are golden and chicken is cooked through.

TIP
Chicken little no more. These are tasty enough for adults to enjoy as an appetizer with a dip or as a main course over dressed greens or pasta.

NUTRITION FACTS

Serving Size: 1/2 breast
(82g)

Calories 210
Calories from Fat 60
Total Fat 7g
Saturated Fat 1.5g
Cholesterol 35mg
Sodium 270mg
Total Carbohydrate 20g
Dietary Fiber 1g
Sugars 2g
Protein 17g

The Movers:
Twelve to
Twenty-four
Months

♥

Anything Kabobs with Chicken

This is a versatile and easy dish for lunch or dinner for all ages. There are a variety of vegetables and proteins that can be chosen to fit your family's taste buds. For vegetarians, the tofu kabobs are a good option. For those who eat meat, there's the chicken option. For a larger quantity and more variety, make both chicken and tofu, as they have the same cooking time and will be ready at once. Drizzle with Sweet and Savory Yogurt Dip (page 147).

MAKES 4 SERVINGS

MARINADE

1½ tablespoons natural, low-sodium soy sauce (tamari)

1½ tablespoons honey

1 tablespoon expeller pressed canola oil

1 scallion or several chives, chopped

1 tablespoon organic orange juice

1 tablespoon freshly squeezed lemon juice

KABOBS

9 ounces boneless, skinless organic chicken breasts, cubed

8 organic cherry tomatoes

8 organic mushrooms

8 mini organic bell peppers or 1 medium organic bell pepper, cut into chunks (about 1 cup) or other vegetable favorites such as baby corn, cut zucchini or broccoli florets

To make marinade: Whisk all ingredients in a small glass or plastic bowl.

To make kabobs: Place chicken in a large glass dish. Pour marinade over chicken. Let chicken marinate in the refrigerator for 30 minutes or longer. Meanwhile, soak 4 wooden or bamboo skewers in cold water for at least 30 minutes.

Thread chicken and vegetables onto skewers, alternating as desired. Place kabobs on a lightly greased baking sheet or broiler pan and transfer to a hot grill or to the oven set on broil. Cook for 5 to 6

EGG FREE

NUTRITION FACTS

Serving Size: 1 kebob (196g)

Calories 180
Calories from Fat 50
Total Fat 6g
Saturated Fat 1g
Cholesterol 50mg
Sodium 250mg
Total Carbohydrate 12g
Dietary Fiber 2g
Sugars 9g
Protein 21g

the
petit
appetit
COOKBOOK
♥

minutes on one side, then turn and cook an additional 4 to 6 minutes on the other, or until cooked through and browned.

VARIATION

Anything Kabobs with Tofu: Substitute 9 ounces cubed, firm organic tofu for the chicken. Marinate tofu for 1 hour or longer. Finish as directed for chicken.

TIPS

Don't forget baby. This meal can be for all ages. Instead of marinating chicken, set aside some to cook on a plain skewer for Explorers and Independents. For Explorers, you can puree chicken and vegetables when finished. And for Independents, chop into small pieces that they can pick up.

Tofu tip. After cutting tofu, blot with a clean kitchen towel or paper towel to remove moisture. This will allow the tofu to soak up more flavors from the marinade, as well as become a bit crunchy.

SERVING SUGGESTIONS

- Let older children carefully help remove skewers and eat with fingers.

- Remove kabob pieces from skewers and arrange in pita bread with greens and favorite spread or dressing. Kabobs go great with Sweet and Savory Yogurt Dip (page 147).

- Remove kabob pieces from skewers and arrange in lettuce leaves. Roll up and secure with toothpick.

- Remove pieces and serve over rice, couscous, or your child's favorite shaped pasta.

NUTRITION FACTS

Serving Size: 1 fillet (115g)

Calories   170
Calories from Fat   60
Total Fat   7g
Saturated Fat   1g
Cholesterol   55mg
Sodium   320mg
Total Carbohydrate   2g
Dietary Fiber   0g
Sugars   1g
Protein   23g

Salmon Filets

This is a quick and easy way to introduce young ones to fish. Coho salmon is usually milder tasting than King salmon, and the soy sauce lends a bit of sweetness.

MAKES 4 SERVINGS

4 (about 4-ounce) wild Coho salmon fillets, skinless and boneless

SAUCE

2 tablespoons natural, low-sodium soy sauce (tamari)

2 tablespoons organic orange juice

2 teaspoons expeller pressed canola oil

1 teaspoon sesame seeds (optional)

Preheat oven to 400°F. Place greased wire rack in center of baking dish lined with foil. Place salmon fillets on rack. Whisk together all sauce ingredients in a small bowl. Brush fillets with sauce. Bake fillets for 12 to 15 minutes, or until fish flakes with a fork.

TIP

Go wild. Unlike farmed-raised salmon, wild salmon does not have any dyes or artificial coloring added to the fish.

Beet Salad

Home-cooked beets are so much richer than the canned version. These are easy to prepare and very versatile. Beets make a good side dish for roasted meats, or tossed over greens and served with soup or stew.

MAKES 10 SERVINGS

4 large (6- to 8-ounce) organic beets, scrubbed

1 tablespoon balsamic vinegar

1 tablespoon extra-virgin olive oil

Sea salt (optional)

¾ cup thinly shredded fresh mint leaves

Preheat oven to 350°F. Trim beets of root and tips and pierce skin with a knife. Wrap beets together in foil and place in a baking pan. Bake for 45 to 60 minutes, or until fork tender. Remove beets from oven and let cool.

When cool enough to handle, peel skin from beets using fingers or paring knife. Cut beets into 1-inch chunks and put into a medium bowl (see note below). Add vinegar, oil, and a pinch of salt, if using. Add mint to beets and toss. Salad can be served warm or cold.

NOTE

If making beets for baby, remove a small portion before adding spices and puree in a food processor until desired texture.

TIP

Turning beet red! Be aware when making and eating beets that the juice may stain clothing. Keep toddlers at the table rather than roaming around and making red fingerprints on your walls.

NUTRITION FACTS

Serving Size: 3 ounces (85g)

Calories 50
Calories from Fat 15
Total Fat 1.5g
Saturated Fat 0g
Cholesterol 0mg
Sodium 85mg
Total Carbohydrate 8g
Dietary Fiber 2g
Sugars 7g
Protein 1g

The Movers:
Twelve to
Twenty-four
Months

♥

NUTRITION FACTS

Serving Size: ½ baguette
with egg and cheese (97g)

Calories   240
Calories from Fat   140
Total Fat   15g
Saturated Fat   8g
Cholesterol   240mg
Sodium   230mg
Total Carbohydrate   14g
Dietary Fiber less than   1g
Sugars   1g
Protein   12g

Happy Breakfast Sandwich

There are many fast-food breakfast sandwiches. Save time, money, and calories at the drive-thru and create your family's favorite on-the-go morning meal.

MAKES 2 SERVINGS

2 cage-free, organic eggs

1 tablespoon unsalted butter

1 (6-inch) baguette or English muffin

1 or 2 slices Swiss cheese

Preheat oven to 375°F. Beat eggs in a small bowl. Heat a small pan over medium heat and add ½ tablespoon of the butter. When butter is melted, pour eggs into pan, and cook on medium heat, stirring with a spatula or wooden spoon, until firm, about 2 minutes. Split baguette and butter with remaining ½ tablespoon butter. Assemble sandwich with egg and cheese and toast open-faced in oven until cheese is melted, about 3 minutes.

TIP

Happy meals every day. A happy meal can be any food or meal activity that pleases your child. A breakfast sandwich shared with a parent in a park can be much more fun than any toy surprise.

Celebration Cupcakes

Whether you're celebrating a birthday, Valentine's Day, or simply a Sunday, these cupcakes are a welcome treat for any occasion. This recipe was adapted from the Children with Diabetes Web site. You'd never know this recipe has half the sugar as most other cupcake recipes.

MAKES 18 CUPCAKES

1 cup organic whole-wheat flour

1 cup unbleached all-purpose flour

½ cup organic wheat germ

1½ teaspoons baking soda

½ teaspoon baking powder

1 teaspoon ground cinnamon

¼ teaspoon dried ground ginger

⅛ teaspoon ground allspice

¾ cup buttermilk

1 cup unsweetened organic applesauce or Apple Puree (page 59)

½ cup unsalted butter, softened

½ cup organic sugar

1 large cage-free, organic egg

FROSTING

4 ounces (½ cup) cream cheese, softened

4 tablespoons unsalted butter, softened

2 tablespoons honey

TO DECORATE

Fresh berries, colored sugars, candles, chocolate or butterscotch chips, or flowers

Heat oven to 350°F. Line a muffin pan with baking liners or grease cups to prevent sticking. In a medium bowl, combine flours, wheat germ, baking soda, baking powder, cinnamon, ginger, and allspice. Combine buttermilk and applesauce in a small bowl. In a large bowl with an electric mixer on medium speed, beat butter and sugar until light and fluffy. Add egg to butter mixture and continue to beat. Alternately add flour mixture and buttermilk mixture and beat to combine.

The Movers:
Twelve to
Twenty-four
Months

♥

Divide batter among muffin cups and bake 25 minutes, or until set. Cool muffins in pan on a wire rack.

To make frosting: Mix together all ingredients in a medium bowl until smooth. When cupcakes are completely cool, remove from pan and frost. Decorate as desired.

TIP

Artistic touch. Toddlers will enjoy helping frost and decorate these cupcakes. If you do not want all the cupcakes decorated with a child's hand, make a double batch to please everyone.

Crunchy Frozen Bananas

Believe it or not, the inspiration for this recipe came from a box of Cheerios, although there are many options for providing the crunch on these tasty bananas. This is a cool and healthy treat for children and adults.

MAKES 8 SERVINGS

4 ripe, firm, large organic bananas

1½ cups or 1 (12-ounce) container organic whole-milk yogurt, any flavor

3 cups cereal (toasted Os, wheat germ, or corn flakes)

Peel and cut bananas in half crosswise. Insert a wooden stick with rounded ends into cut ends of bananas. Place yogurt in a small bowl. Sprinkle cereal on a plate or waxed paper. Dip bananas in yogurt to cover. Then roll yogurt-covered bananas in cereal to coat. Place finished bananas on baking sheet or plate and place in the freezer for about 1 hour, or until firm.

TIP

Freeze, please! You can store these to serve anytime. Just wrap each banana in waxed or parchment paper, and place in a freezer bag. Label, date, and store in the freezer for up to 1 month.

NUTRITION FACTS

Serving Size: 1 banana
(122g)

Calories 150
Calories from Fat 10
Total Fat 1.5g
Saturated Fat 0g
Cholesterol 5mg
Sodium 130mg
Total Carbohydrate 32g
Dietary Fiber 3g
Sugars 16g
Protein 4g

The Movers:
Twelve to
Twenty-four
Months

♥

Baby Ginger Carrots

Many children love carrots. My twelve-month-old friend David liked this recipe because he was going through an orange stage. Cooking until just tender or al dente makes these carrots easy to eat, but they still have some texture and firmness.

MAKES 3 TO 4 SERVINGS

1 (10-ounce) bag organic baby carrots, or 3 regular-size organic carrots, peeled

½ cup organic vegetable broth

2 tablespoons freshly squeezed lemon juice

½ teaspoon freshly grated ginger (about 1-inch piece)

1 tablespoon chopped fresh parsley

If using regular-size carrots, cut into equal-size rounds or matchsticks. Bring carrots and broth to a boil in a small saucepan over medium heat. Cover and simmer over medium-low heat until carrots are tender, but not mushy, 15 minutes. Drain liquid, add lemon juice, ginger, and parsley, and toss together.

TIP

Shortcut baby. If you don't have the time or energy to peel and cut carrots, buy bagged, peeled baby carrots. You can find these in the produce department at most supermarkets.

NUTRITION FACTS

Serving Size: 3 ounces (85g)

Calories   30
Calories from Fat   0
Total Fat   0g
Saturated Fat   0g
Cholesterol   0mg
Sodium   60mg
Total Carbohydrate   7g
Dietary Fiber   1g
Sugars   4g
Protein   1g

the
petit
appetit
COOKBOOK
♥

Heart-y Yogurt Pancakes

In honor of Valentine's Day, here is a great breakfast (or anytime treat) to express your love with heart-shaped pancakes. Top hearts with fresh berries, yogurt, and/or maple syrup.

MAKES 12 (4- TO 5-INCH HEART) PANCAKES

1 cage-free, organic egg, slightly beaten

⅔ cup organic whole-milk yogurt (see tip below)

⅔ cup organic milk or soy milk

¾ cup unbleached all-purpose flour

¼ teaspoon salt

In a medium bowl, mix together egg and yogurt until smooth. Add milk, flour, and salt. Mix until batter is smooth. If batter is too thin, add more flour.

Heat a nonstick skillet over medium heat. Spray with cooking spray, or drizzle enough oil to lightly coat the pan. Drop heaping tablespoons of batter into pan to create heart shapes. Leave enough room around each heart to turn easily. These will be free-form, not perfect. Older children may even want to help with this task.

Cook for 1 to 2 minutes and watch for bubbles to form on the surface before flipping with a spatula. Cook another 1 to 2 minutes on other side until cooked through, and lightly browned on each side.

TIP

In the pink. If you want light pink hearts, choose a strawberry or raspberry flavor yogurt as the batter will take on a bit of color. Pancakes will also be sweeter than using plain yogurt.

NUTRITION FACTS

Serving Size: 2 pancakes (80g)

Calories 110
Calories from Fat 15
Total Fat 2g
Saturated Fat 0.5g
Cholesterol 40mg
Sodium 430mg
Total Carbohydrate 18g
Dietary Fiber 0g
Sugars 4g
Protein 5g

The Movers:
Twelve to
Twenty-four
Months

♥

Mango Tango Smoothie

This is a sweet and frosty morning breakfast or anytime snack packed with vitamin C, protein, and potassium for an active toddler.

MAKES 2 SERVINGS

1 medium organic mango, cut into chunks (about 1 cup)
1 frozen ripe organic banana, cut into chunks
½ cup organic orange juice
½ cup vanilla or plain organic whole-milk yogurt

Put all ingredients in a blender and process until smooth, about 30 seconds.

TIP

Frozen bananas: Peel banana, wrap in waxed paper, and seal in a self-sealing freezer bag. Be sure to label and date the contents. Freezing the fruit for smoothies eliminates the need for ice and is a convenient shortcut when you want to prepare a frozen treat. Plus, the smoothie won't be watered down or have any surprise icy chunks.

NUTRITION FACTS

Serving Size: 1 cup (252g)

Calories 130
Calories from Fat 10
Total Fat 1g
Saturated Fat 0.5g
Cholesterol 5mg
Sodium 45mg
Total Carbohydrate 28g
Dietary Fiber 3g
Sugars 21g
Protein 5g

Multigrain Scones

These are popular at family gatherings of young and old alike. A few of my little tasters loved to lick the topping off before finishing their scones.

MAKES 12 SCONES

1 cage-free, organic egg

½ cup packed organic light brown sugar

5 tablespoons expeller pressed canola oil

½ cup organic rolled oats

¼ cup organic wheat germ

1½ cups organic whole-wheat flour

½ teaspoon salt

1 tablespoon baking powder

½ teaspoon ground cinnamon

¼ teaspoon grated lemon zest

½ cup soy milk (see note below)

TOPPING (OPTIONAL)

1 tablespoon fresh lemon juice

3 tablespoons confectioner's sugar

Preheat oven to 375°F. In a large bowl, whisk together egg, sugar, and oil to make a thick paste. In a separate bowl, combine oats, wheat germ, wheat flour, salt, baking powder, cinnamon, and zest. Slowly beat the flour mixture into the egg mixture to create a thick dough. Stir in the milk and beat well.

On a lightly greased baking pan, drop mounds of dough about 2 inches apart. You may round the edges with your fingers or a spoon if desired. Bake about 15 minutes, or until golden crust forms on top of scone and dough is dry to touch. Remove pan and let cool for 10 minutes.

For topping: In a small bowl, combine lemon juice and sugar until sugar is dissolved. Drizzle over top of warm scones.

NOTE

Got milk? Any milk can be substituted above: cow's milk, flavored soy milk, or rice milk all work well.

The Movers: Twelve to Twenty-four Months

♥

the
petit
appetit
COOKBOOK
♥

Pumpkin Polenta

This is one of the few times when canned vegetables are suggested instead of fresh. Canned pumpkin has the same nutritional value as fresh. Using canned also means this recipe can be made anytime, not just at Halloween.

MAKES 8 SERVINGS

2 cups milk

1 cup canned pumpkin

½ teaspoon ground cinnamon

½ teaspoon ground ginger

¼ teaspoon freshly grated or ground nutmeg

⅛ teaspoon salt

½ cup organic polenta

1 tablespoon unsalted butter

1 tablespoon maple syrup

Combine first 6 ingredients in a medium saucepan, and bring to boil over medium heat. Slowly pour in polenta and whisk to combine. Be careful because hot polenta may bubble and spit. Reduce heat and simmer for 5 minutes, whisking occasionally until thick. Remove saucepan from heat and stir in butter and syrup.

Tofu Fries

I couldn't fool Eli, a fourteen-month-old client who liked french fries, into believing these were *real* french fries. However, he did come around and now likes both french and tofu fries. Be sure to use firm tofu and remove as much moisture as possible so these fries bake crisp. These tofu fries puff up when cooked.

MAKES ABOUT 24 FRIES; 4 SERVINGS

1 (1-pound) package extra-firm organic tofu
Salt and black pepper, to taste

DIPPING OPTIONS:

ketchup, mustard, Asian pepper sauce, soy sauce

Preheat broiler. Drain and rinse tofu with water. Slice tofu lengthwise into 3 equal slices. Dry each side of tofu with paper towels to remove as much moisture as possible. Cut each of the 3 slices into equal-size strips. Place each strip onto a parchment-lined baking sheet. Sprinkle with salt and pepper.

Broil tofu until firm and golden, 15 to 20 minutes. Check every few minutes and turn halfway through cooking. Dip into sauce of choice, if desired.

NUTRITION FACTS

Serving Size: 6 fries (78g)

Calories 80
Calories from Fat 45
Total Fat 5g
Saturated Fat 1g
Cholesterol 0mg
Sodium 10mg
Total Carbohydrate 1g
Dietary Fiber 1g
Sugars 0g
Protein 10g

The Movers:
Twelve to
Twenty-four
Months

♥

Spring Spread

This was a favorite of mine while a freshman at U.C. Davis. On a nice sunny day, I would stop at the coffeehouse and order a wheat bagel with spring spread to take with me to eat on the quad. Years later I was cooking for a two-year-old whose mother was worried she wasn't eating enough vegetables. She loved cream cheese, so my college favorite became her morning breakfast. Try using different vegetables, such as grated zucchini or finely chopped celery, for variety. Besides for bagels, this spread doubles as a dip for carrot and celery sticks.

MAKES ABOUT ½ CUP

4 ounces organic cream cheese, whipped or softened

2 tablespoons grated organic carrot

2 tablespoon finely diced organic red bell pepper

1 tablespoon finely diced green chives

1 teaspoon chopped fresh dill, thyme, or rosemary, or combination

1 teaspoon freshly squeezed lemon or lime juice

Mix all ingredients together in a small bowl with a rubber spatula until creamy.

TIP

Texture detectives. You may want to chop the vegetables more finely depending on your child's issues with texture. For particular eaters, you can process the mixture in a food processor so it's tougher to pick out the veggies.

CRACKER CUT-OUTS

For fun and unique crackers, get out your cookie cutters. Cut shapes in soft wheat tortillas and place on a baking sheet. Bake the shapes in a 325°F oven for about 10 minutes, or until golden and crisp.

NUTRITION FACTS

Serving Size: 2 tablespoons (30g)

Calories from Fat 70
Total Fat 8g
Saturated Fat 5g
Cholesterol 25mg
Sodium 65mg
Total Carbohydrate 1g
Dietary Fiber 0g
Sugars 0g
Protein 2g

the
petit
appetit
COOKBOOK
♥

Tangy Barbecue Sauce

There are lots of bottled sauces on the market, but homemade is much tastier without all the additives and preservatives. Baste your ribs, chicken, or burgers with this sauce at your next barbecue. Or use as a dip for chicken strips.

MAKES ABOUT 4 CUPS

½ (16-ounce) carton Pomi chopped tomatoes
½ small organic yellow onion, finely chopped (about ¼ cup)
1 tablespoon Worcestershire sauce
2 teaspoons molasses
Sea salt and black pepper, to taste

Combine all ingredients in a medium saucepan. Bring to a boil and cook until mixture is thick, stirring frequently with a wooden spoon.

TIP
You say tomato, I say Pomi tomato. Fresh tomatoes aren't always so sweet if not in season. Pomi tomatoes are fresh, cooked tomatoes available all year long. They come packaged as chopped, whole, and sauce varieties. You can find them at most supermarkets. But look for them packaged in a carton, not in a can.

NUTRITION FACTS
Serving Size: 2 tablespoons
(30g)

Calories   10
Calories from Fat   0
Total Fat   0g
Saturated Fat   0g
Cholesterol   0mg
Sodium   45mg
Total Carbohydrate   2g
Dietary Fiber   0g
Sugars   1g
Protein   0g

The Movers:
Twelve to
Twenty-four
Months

♥

EGG FREE

VEGAN

NUTRITION FACTS

Serving Size: 1 slice (55g)

Calories 190
Calories from Fat 25
Total Fat 2.5g
Saturated Fat 0g
Cholesterol 0mg
Sodium 10mg
Total Carbohydrate 38g
Dietary Fiber 7g
Sugars 3g
Protein 8g

Whole Wheat Bread

At ten weeks old, my son, Jonas, was entranced while watching me knead this dough. I would sit on the kitchen floor next to his bouncy chair and talk to him all the while playing with a big dough ball. It was a bit messy sometimes, but he was very entertained.

MAKES 8 SERVINGS

1 package (1 tablespoon) active dry yeast
¾ cup lukewarm water
⅛ cup mild molasses
1 tablespoon expeller pressed canola oil
3¼ cups organic whole-wheat flour, plus extra for kneading

In a large mixing bowl dissolve yeast in lukewarm water. Add molasses and oil and stir with a rubber spatula to combine. Set aside until mixture bubbles and foams, 5 to 6 minutes. Add flour to mixture, 1 cup at a time, stirring with a rubber spatula.

Once flour has been incorporated turn dough onto floured surface and knead 8 to 10 minutes. Alternatively, you can mix and knead dough with a stand mixer fitted with a dough hook. Wash your hands and test doneness by inserting a dry thumb. If it comes out clean and dough springs back, it's kneaded well.

Put dough into a greased 8 × 4-inch loaf pan. Cover with a damp cloth and set aside for 45 to 60 minutes, until dough has risen.

Preheat oven to 350°F. Place bread on center rack of oven and bake for 30 minutes, or until crust is golden and sounds hollow when thumped. Cool in pan for 10 minutes and turn out on a wire rack to cool completely.

TIP

All you knead. Everyone loves homemade bread; however, not everyone wants to buy and store a pricey bread machine. This recipe only needs a few ingredients and your hands to make whole-wheat bread for sandwiches and spreads.

St. Pat's Spinach Pesto

This recipe is a twist on the typical basil pesto, with more vitamins and nutrients. This is also different in that it is nut-free, so no need to worry about potential allergies for little ones. Go green and serve this sauce on pizza or tossed with your children's favorite pasta shape for a festive St. Patrick's Day dinner.

MAKES ABOUT 1 CUP

3 cups packed, washed, and stemmed organic spinach leaves

1 medium garlic clove, minced

½ teaspoon salt

¼ teaspoon freshly ground black pepper

⅓ cup virgin olive oil

⅓ cup freshly grated Parmesan cheese

Place spinach, garlic, salt, and pepper in a food processor fitted with a steel blade. Process until chopped and combined. With machine running, add oil in a steady stream and process until smooth, about 45 seconds. Scrape down halfway through processing. Add cheese and process just until blended.

TIP

Get the grit out. An easy way to wash spinach is to fill your sink with cool water and plunge the spinach leaves in the water. The silt, sand, and grit will sink to the bottom of the water and the leaves will float on the top.

NUTRITION FACTS

Serving Size: 2 tablespoons (30g)

Calories 100
Calories from Fat 90
Total Fat 10g
Saturated Fat 2g
Cholesterol 5mg
Sodium 150mg
Total Carbohydrate 2g
Dietary Fiber less than 1g
Sugars 0g
Protein 2g

The Movers:
Twelve to
Twenty-four
Months

♥

Chapter 11

The Shakers: Two to Three Years

Introduction Map

(Can eat all Movers' food, plus the following)

FOODS APPROPRIATE	REASON	CONSISTENCY/TEXTURE
Liquids: whole cow's milk, water, soy and rice beverages, juice	Need calcium for growing bones	
Family meals and snacks, including dips and sandwiches	Taste a variety of foods and flavors. Need for fuel with activity level.	Child will self-feed, but need help cutting.

READY?

If you want to shake things up, invite a two-year-old to dinner. They are full of surprises, positive and negative. Up until now their culinary journey may have gone smoothly, trying new foods and gaining better eating skills. However, some children at this stage will refuse to eat even their past favorite foods, in order to gain some independence and test their boundaries. They have little control over most of their daily activities, and growing up means wanting some freedoms and choices.

SET?

If you provide different foods, some familiar and some unfamiliar, they are likely to eat something. If they do not eat any of the options, that is their choice. Nutritionists advise to let them wait until the next meal or snacktime rather than prepare special foods. Do not allow the table to become a battleground, if possible. This is a test of wills—yours and your child's. Some will push, beg, and whine to get what they want. Parents have to decide what kind of eating habits and dining atmosphere they want to develop.

Be consistent with your eating and mealtime rituals. Children will have other influences around them: friends, relatives, day care, and babysitters. Ask these caregivers to follow your feeding instructions and rules as well to maintain healthy eating habits, even when you are away from your child.

GO!

And I do mean go! You need to be on your toes to keep up with this age. Keep them engaged with a variety of foods and experiences in the kitchen. Here you'll find quick snack and travel recipes to sustain these active bodies and curious minds, as well as meals the entire family can enjoy together.

Mealtimes and cooking will be about more than just food and eating. The Shakers may be able to ask questions and engage in (as well as disrupt) the food preparation process. There are many lessons to be learned in the kitchen—numbers, colors, vocabulary, and more. See Chapter 4, Parenting in the Kitchen, for more ideas.

STOP FORCING AND BRIBING WITH FOOD

Once your child can communicate that he does not want any more, do not push him to eat more. Children will eat when they are hungry, no matter what the food is. My clients always tell me their active toddlers won't and don't eat. However, if you look at their total day and mark their intake of food, they're eating more than you realize. See Appendix B for a helpful log. A snack here and there and bites on the go all add up during the day. If your child is healthy, active, and gaining weight, he is getting enough to eat. A healthy child will not starve. Alternatively, some children may gain too much weight. Possibly their diet is too abundant in empty calories with juices, sugary snacks, and processed foods. If your child is not thriving and you are concerned, consult your pediatrician.

Bribing children with food and candy is a common topic at my workshops. This is a difficult habit to break. I know parents who give their children sweets for all types of tasks: using the "big potty," going to the doctor, getting in their car seat, and even being nice to their siblings. Rather than rewarding good habits and long-term behavior, parents give in to avoid fights, tantrums, and tears. Rewards should not be tied to food, even if the food is healthy, as this can create negative food relationships when children get older. Why not reward behavior with time spent as a family at the park or zoo? I have one client who puts a happy face on the refrigerator for her daughter, Ella's, accomplishments. Ella can save those earned happy faces and turn them in for a special play date with her grandma.

TRIP TO THE DENTIST

Now is the time to visit the dentist for a checkup. A soft child's toothbrush is effective for keeping teeth free of plaque and starts healthy brushing habits. According to Jon Orinstil, D.D.S., the best way to protect your child's teeth is to avoid sticky, chewy foods and sugary liquids. Your dentist may also recommend fluoride additives to keep children's teeth free from decay.

The Shakers: Recipes

Lee's Lentil Veggie Stew

This is a hearty stew for all ages, rich in flavor, iron, protein, fiber, and vitamins. Even my husband, who is not a lentil fan, likes this sweet and savory recipe. I named it after him instead of calling it "I Knew You'd Like It" stew.

MAKES ABOUT 4 CUPS

1 tablespoon virgin olive oil

1 organic celery stalk, chopped (about ¼ cup)

½ medium organic yellow onion, chopped (about ½ cup)

1 medium organic carrot, peeled and chopped (about ¾ cup)

1 small garlic clove, minced

¾ cup dried organic lentils

1 quart organic vegetable broth

1 tablespoon chopped fresh oregano

1 tablespoon chopped fresh parsley

1 teaspoon chopped fresh thyme

1 medium organic sweet potato, peeled and chopped (about 1 cup)

2 teaspoons cider vinegar

Plain organic whole-milk yogurt, for topping

Heat the oil in a large stockpot over medium-high heat. Add vegetables and sauté for 6 to 8 minutes, stirring frequently, until onion is translucent. Add garlic and lentils and cook for 2 minutes, stirring constantly. Add broth. Bring to a boil and reduce heat to low.

Simmer stew for 30 to 40 minutes, stirring occasionally, until lentils are tender. (If making for baby, remove portion to puree.) Add herbs and vinegar and cook for an additional 10 minutes. Serve steaming hot bowls of stew with a dollop of yogurt on top.

NOTE
This recipe is suitable for Independents. Before adding spices, remove desired amount and puree in a food processor until smooth or mash with a fork to create more texture.

NUTRITION FACTS
Serving Size: 1 cup (383g)

Calories 240
Calories from Fat 35
Total Fat 4g
Saturated Fat 0.5g
Cholesterol 0mg
Sodium 960mg
Total Carbohydrate 41g
Dietary Fiber 11g
Sugars 9g
Protein 11g

The Shakers:
Two to Three
Years

♥

Wild Polenta

The combination of mushrooms, tomatoes, and goat cheese is a tasty one. You can cut polenta into standard squares or shake things up and use a cookie cutter to create unexpected shapes.

MAKES 8 SERVINGS

4 cups water

1½ cups organic polenta

2 tablespoons unsalted butter

2 tablespoon olive oil

2 cups sliced organic wild mushrooms (porcini, portobello, crimini, or combination)

½ cup chopped organic tomatoes

¼ teaspoon sea salt

¼ teaspoon black pepper

3 ounces goat cheese

Line an 8-inch square shallow baking pan with parchment paper. Bring water to a boil over high heat in a large saucepan. Add the polenta, stirring constantly. Bring back to a boil, and cook until polenta is thick and smooth, stirring constantly, about 3 minutes. Spoon polenta into prepared pan and spread evenly with a rubber spatula.

Preheat the oven to 400°F. Melt butter in a medium skillet over medium heat. Add oil and mushrooms and sauté until golden and aromatic, 3 to 5 minutes. Stir in tomatoes, salt, and pepper and cook until hot.

Turn out polenta onto a cutting board. Peel away the parchment paper and cut polenta into squares. Put squares in a large, shallow ovenproof dish and cover with mushroom-tomato mixture. Sprinkle goat cheese on polenta squares and bake for about 20 minutes, until heated through.

EGG FREE

GLUTEN FREE

SUGAR FREE

VEGETARIAN

NUTRITION FACTS

Serving Size: ⅛ of dish

Calories   120
Calories from Fat   90
Total Fat   10g
Saturated Fat   4.5g
Cholesterol   15mg
Sodium   130mg
Total Carbohydrate   5g
Dietary Fiber less than   1g
Sugars   1g
Protein   4g

the
petit
appetit
COOKBOOK
♥

TIP

Polenta quick. Polenta is an easy grain to cook; it can be ready in minutes. Polenta is sold in boxes, in bulk, or even ready-made. If using ready-made, skip to the second step.

Roasted Red Pepper Puree

Bell peppers come in a variety of bright colors: red, orange, yellow, and green. Roasted peppers are delicious additions to sandwiches, salads, and pastas. This recipe uses red peppers for a sweet and intense puree that's great for pasta, dips, or spreading on your favorite sandwiches or roll-ups.

SERVINGS 15

2 large (6- to 8-ounce) organic red bell peppers

Preheat oven broiler to high. Line a roasting pan with aluminum foil. Place whole peppers on pan and roast for 12 to 15 minutes, turning every 3 minutes to be sure all sides are charred. Remove pan from oven and let peppers sit until cool enough to handle, about 15 minutes. The steam inside the peppers will make the skins easy to remove. Pull off skins using your fingers and cut peppers in half lengthwise to remove seeds and stems. Cut halves in half.

Place peppers in a food processor fitted with a steel blade; no additional liquid is required. Process until pureed.

TIP

Peeling peppers. If you don't want to wait for the peppers to cool after roasting, you can place the peppers in a paper grocery bag and fold over to close. Place the bag in your sink to avoid a mess. This speeds up the steaming process and makes the peppers peel easily.

Simply Salsa

This is a basic tomato salsa recipe, good for dipping and topping all kinds of foods, including chips, tacos, burritos, stuffed potatoes, vegetables, and more. Medical research suggests that the consumption of lycopene, the stuff that makes tomatoes red, may help prevent certain cancers and heart disease. So everyone should feel free to dip away.

MAKES ABOUT 2 CUPS

1 pound vine-ripened organic tomatoes, chopped (about 2 cups)

½ small organic yellow onion, minced (about ¼ cup)

½ cup minced fresh cilantro

2 teaspoons freshly squeezed lime juice

½ teaspoon sea salt

¼ teaspoon black pepper

Combine all ingredients in a small bowl and mash with the back of a fork to release juices and mix flavors. Serve right away or hold in the refrigerator for up to 2 to 3 days.

TIP

Guac this way. Add this salsa to your baby's Avocado Puree (page 62) and you have an easy guacamole.

NUTRITION FACTS

Serving Size: 2 tablespoons (30g)

Calories   5
Calories from Fat   0
Total Fat   0g
Saturated Fat   0g
Cholesterol   0mg
Sodium   70mg
Total Carbohydrate   1g
Dietary Fiber   0g
Sugars   1g
Protein   0g

The Shakers:
Two to Three
Years

♥

Orange Frosty

This is a refreshing pick-me-up snack loaded with vitamin C. Sometimes kids enjoy the yogurt and juice cubes on their own, before you can even make the final frosty. If you freeze extra cubes, this treat can be ready whenever your children are.

MAKES ABOUT 2 CUPS

¾ cup plain organic whole-milk yogurt
¾ cup organic orange juice
½ cup unfiltered, pasteurized organic apple juice

Divide yogurt among 6 ice cube tray sections. Pour orange juice into remaining 6 sections, and freeze. When frozen, pop out all cubes and place in a blender with apple juice. Blend until combined and slushy.

NUTRITION FACTS

Serving Size: I cup (240g)

Calories   210
Calories from Fat   30
Total Fat   3g
Saturated Fat   2g
Cholesterol   10mg
Sodium   60mg
Total Carbohydrate   42g
Dietary Fiber   0g
Sugars   11g
Protein   4g

the
petit
appetit
COOKBOOK
♥

Kiwi-Banana Freeze

Kiwifruit have a brown fuzzy skin outside and beautiful green flesh inside. Because of the furry skin, the French call kiwis *souris végétales* or "vegetable mice." Your child will enjoy the bright color and fresh flavor of this cool treat; you may need to strain the seeds for some precocious little mice.

MAKES ABOUT 2 CUPS

2 large (2- to 3-ounce) kiwifruit

1 medium organic banana, frozen and cut into large chunks

⅓ cup Apple Puree (page 59) or unsweetened organic applesauce

Combine all ingredients in a blender and process until smooth. If necessary, strain seeds through a fine mesh sieve.

TIP

C-me. Kiwifruit are rich in vitamin C, containing pound for pound ten times that of lemons.

The Shakers:
Two to Three
Years

♥

NUTRITION FACTS

Serving Size: I bar (73g)

Calories   260
Calories from Fat   100
Total Fat   11g
Saturated Fat   1.5g
Cholesterol   45mg
Sodium   20mg
Total Carbohydrate   36g
Dietary Fiber   5g
Sugars   15g
Protein   9g

Granola Bars

Granola bars are a good way to bring along granola without the mess. This makes an easy alternative to buying store-bought granola bars with added sugars and preservatives. You can also create your own flavor of bars by changing the fruit spread. I've found berry spreads to be the most popular.

MAKES ABOUT 9 SQUARES

2 cage-free, organic eggs

2 cups Fruit-Free Granola (page 193) or store bought

¼ teaspoon vanilla extract

⅓ cup all-fruit raspberry spread

Preheat oven to 350°F. In a medium bowl, slightly beat eggs. Add granola and stir with a rubber spatula to combine. Pour mixture into an 8-inch square glass baking dish. Carefully spread the raspberry spread over granola. Bake for 15 minutes, or until set and golden brown. Cut into squares and remove with a spatula to cool on wire rack.

TIP

Pass on the jelly. Jelly is full of added sugars. However, in the same aisle at the supermarket you'll find all-fruit spreads. These are the whole fruit and nothing but the fruit.

Carrot-Cilantro Soup

Here's a great way to use baby's leftover carrot puree. This soup will become a sweet and creamy comfort food for the whole family.

MAKES 6 CUPS

2 tablespoons unsalted butter

1 medium organic yellow onion, chopped, about 1 cup

1 garlic clove, minced

2 cups (16 ounces) organic vegetable broth

1 recipe Carrot Puree (page 91)

1½ cups organic whole milk

⅓ cup finely chopped fresh cilantro

Sea salt and white pepper, to taste

Heat butter in a heavy stockpot over medium heat. Add onion and garlic and cook over low heat until onion is golden, 6 to 8 minutes. Add broth and carrot puree and bring to a boil. Cover and simmer for 20 minutes. Transfer to a food processor or blender and puree. Return soup to stockpot and stir in the milk and cilantro. Heat over low heat until hot. Season with salt and pepper.

NUTRITION FACTS

Serving Size: 1 cup (225g)

Calories 130
Calories from Fat 50
Total Fat 6g
Saturated Fat 2.5g
Cholesterol 15mg
Sodium 340mg
Total Carbohydrate 17g
Dietary Fiber 2g
Sugars 2g
Protein 3g

The Shakers:
Two to Three
Years

♥

VEGETARIAN

the
petit
appetit
COOKBOOK

♥

Mrs. Barnes's Fish Sticks

Forget about frozen sticks with imposter fish and fake breading. Your child deserves the real thing. Use a mild white fish for this recipe. Serve a variety of dipping options such as ketchup, malt vinegar, and tartar sauce.

MAKES 4 SERVINGS

1 cup milk

1 cage-free, organic egg, slightly beaten

1 cup toasted oat cereal

2 tablespoons unbleached all-purpose flour

¼ teaspoon salt

1 pound skinless, boneless fish fillets (halibut, cod, or tilapia)

¼ cup expeller pressed canola oil

In a shallow dish beat together milk and egg. Put cereal in a food processor and pulse to into crumbs. Or place in a self-sealing plastic bag and crush with a rolling pin. On a flat plate, combine cereal, flour, and salt. Cut fish into 8 equal-size pieces. Dip fish pieces into milk-egg mixture, and then dredge in cereal mixture to coat.

Heat oil in a large nonstick skillet over medium-high heat. Add fish sticks to pan and cook until brown and crispy outside and cooked and flaky inside, 3 to 4 minutes on each side, turning with a spatula. Reduce heat if there is too much splattering. Pat fish sticks with paper towels to soak up any excess oil.

TIP

Everyone has Os. I've discovered that every household with a child under five years old has some brand of toasted Os cereal. You'll be surprised how well your child's favorite cereal performs in recipes that call for bread crumbs, stuffing, or even nuts.

Manny's Lemon Pancakes

Gayle Pirie and John Clark, chef-owners of San Francisco's Foreign Cinema restaurant and coauthors of *Country Egg, City Egg*, developed this recipe to re-create a child comfort food enjoyed on sleepover mornings. This "dramatic egg pancake" is also known as a Dutch Baby.

MAKES 4 SERVINGS

3 cage-free, organic eggs

½ cup organic milk

½ cup unbleached all-purpose flour (see note below)

½ teaspoon salt

2 tablespoons unsalted butter

Juice of ½ lemon

Organic confectioner's sugar, for sprinkling

Preheat the oven to 375°F. Whisk the eggs and milk together. Add the flour and salt and whisk until a smooth batter with tiny bubbles is formed.

Melt butter in a large skillet over medium heat. When the butter is hot and begins to sizzle, add the batter, and remove from heat. Place skillet on center rack of oven and bake for 10 to 12 minutes, or until pancake is light golden and has risen like a soufflé. The edges will be creeping over the rim of the skillet and be nicely browned.

Remove from the oven, sprinkle with lemon juice and a dusting of sugar. Cut pancake into pieces and eat immediately.

ALL-PURPOSE NOT FOR ALL

Not everyone can eat all-purpose wheat flour. I've made this recipe successfully with spelt, gluten-free, and rice flours. Use whichever works with your family's diet and preference.

NUTRITION FACTS

Serving Size: ¼ pancake (95g)

Calories 180
Calories from Fat 90
Total Fat 10g
Saturated Fat 4.5g
Cholesterol 175mg
Sodium 400mg
Total Carbohydrate 14g
Dietary Fiber 0g
Sugars 0g
Protein 7g

The Shakers:
Two to Three
Years

♥

A Dilly of a Vinaigrette

This vinaigrette is great on a main dish salad like the Salad Niçoise (page 188). It also dresses up a simple green salad and wake ups everyday steamed vegetables.

MAKES ABOUT ½ CUP

1 large shallot, minced

1 clove garlic, minced

2 tablespoons freshly squeezed lemon juice

3 tablespoons balsamic vinegar

3 tablespoons rice wine vinegar

¼ cup virgin olive oil

2 tablespoons chopped fresh dill

⅛ teaspoon sea salt

⅛ teaspoon black pepper

Whisk all ingredients together in a small bowl

TIP
Choose firm, dry shallots with well-rounded bulbs about ¾ inches in diameter. The outer skin should be smooth and dry without any shriveling. Avoid spongy bulbs and those that are sprouting.

NUTRITION FACTS

Serving Size: 2 tablespoons
(30g)

Calories   70
Calories from Fat   60
Total Fat   7g
Saturated Fat   1g
Cholesterol   0mg
Sodium   40mg
Total Carbohydrate   3g
Dietary Fiber   0g
Sugars   1g
Protein   0g

the
petit
appetit
COOKBOOK
♥

Greek Frittata

A frittata is an easy, yet elegant dish to serve for friends and family. Adding cous-cous to the frittata makes it heartier and gives the eggs a bit of a crust. Slice the frittata into wedges and your children will think it's an egg pie.

MAKES 6 SERVINGS

½ cup water plus 1 tablespoon water

⅓ cup uncooked organic couscous

½ teaspoon salt

¼ teaspoon black pepper

5 cage-free, organic eggs

2 teaspoons expeller pressed canola oil

⅓ cup slivered oil-packed sun-dried tomatoes

⅓ cup chopped niçoise or kalamata olives

¼ cup diced organic onion

¼ cup grated Parmesan cheese

¼ cup crumbled feta cheese

Preheat oven to 350°F. In a small saucepan, bring the ½ cup water to a boil over medium-high heat. Stir in couscous, remove pan from heat, cover, and let stand for 5 minutes. Fluff and separate with fork.

Combine the 1 tablespoon water, salt, pepper, and eggs in a medium bowl and whisk together. Heat oil in a large ovenproof skillet over medium-high heat. Add tomatoes, olives, and onion and sauté until soft, about 3 minutes. Remove pan from heat and stir in couscous and egg mixture. Level mixture with a rubber spatula. Sprinkle cheeses over top. Bake frittata for 10 minutes, or until set and cooked through. Let stand for 5 minutes. Cut into wedges with a knife or pizza cutter.

NUTRITION FACTS

Serving Size: ⅙ of frittata (111g)

Calories 190
Calories from Fat 80
Total Fat 9g
Saturated Fat 3g
Cholesterol 185mg
Sodium 740mg
Total Carbohydrate 17g
Dietary Fiber 3g
Sugars 6g
Protein 11g

The Shakers:
Two to Three
Years

♥

Fish Tacos

Children enjoy building their own tacos. Give them lots of fresh salsa (page 177) and healthy ingredients to create their own taco masterpiece. This fish option is a welcome change from the usual ground beef or chicken. It is also a great way to quickly reinvent any leftover fish.

MAKES 6 SERVINGS

4 ounces ono or other white fish fillets

Sea salt and black pepper, to taste

1 cup shredded organic cabbage

1 lime, quartered

6 (6-inch) corn tortillas

SAUCE

2 tablespoons plain organic whole-milk yogurt

1 tablespoon minced fresh cilantro

1½ teaspoons freshly squeezed lime juice

1 teaspoon minced organic onion

Preheat oven to 400°F. Season fish with salt and pepper and place on greased rack over foil-lined baking dish. Bake fish for 10 minutes, or until it flakes.

To make the sauce: Whisk all ingredients in a small bowl until creamy.

Arrange fish, cabbage, sauce, lime, and tortillas on a platter and let each person build his own taco masterpiece.

TIP

Fish for baby. Before assembling tacos, remove a portion of fish for baby. Flake into small pieces or puree (see First Fish, page 98).

NUTRITION FACTS

Serving Size: 1 taco (66g)

Calories 90
Calories from Fat 10
Total Fat 1g
Saturated Fat 0g
Cholesterol 20mg
Sodium 30mg
Total Carbohydrate 16g
Dietary Fiber 3g
Sugars 0g
Protein 6g

the
petit
appetit
COOKBOOK

Cauliflower Gratin

My husband, who says he doesn't like cauliflower, was surprised by how much he loves this dish. The gratin is a fancy word for something baked with cheese, which will please your toddler, and hopefully your husband. This dish makes a great side to grilled meats, as well as a hearty lunch entrée with a green salad.

MAKES 12 SERVINGS

1 (1-pound) head organic cauliflower, separated into equal-size florets
2 tablespoons unsalted butter
1 small organic yellow onion, thinly sliced (about ½ cup)
⅓ cup organic milk
½ cup dry bread crumbs
⅓ cup grated Parmesan cheese
½ teaspoon freshly grated or ground nutmeg
¼ teaspoon salt

Preheat oven to 400°F. Steam cauliflower according to method described on page 85 for Cauliflower Puree.

Heat a large ovenproof skillet over medium heat and melt 1 tablespoon of the butter until foamy. Add onion and cook until golden, 5 to 6 minutes. Add cauliflower, milk and crumbs to skillet and stir. Be sure cauliflower is coated with crumbs and onion is distributed. Sprinkle cheese over cauliflower mixture and top with pieces of butter. Put skillet in oven and bake for 20 minutes, or until cheese is melted and golden and crumbs are crisp.

THAT'S CRUMBLY

Make your own bread crumbs in no time at all. Get a loaf of day-old French or sourdough bread (a baguette or large round works well) and grate it with a box grater to make crumbs. Of course, you can buy commercially packaged bread crumbs, but read the label, as many are full of preservatives and trans fats.

EGG FREE

SUGAR FREE

VEGETARIAN

NUTRITION FACTS

Serving Size: ¹⁄₁₂ of recipe (83g)

Calories   110
Calories from Fat   50
Total Fat   6g
Saturated Fat   3.5g
Cholesterol   15mg
Sodium   290mg
Total Carbohydrate   8g
Dietary Fiber   2g
Sugars   2g
Protein   7g

The Shakers:
Two to Three
Years

♥

Asparagus Niçoise Salad

This is a great main dish salad for a light weeknight supper or a side dish for a family weekend brunch. If you have hard-cooked eggs on hand, this can be put together in no time.

MAKES 4 SERVINGS

1 small bunch (6 ounces) organic asparagus

2 cage-free, organic eggs

4 cups lightly packed organic arugula

1 (6-ounce) can chunk light tuna, drained

1 cup pitted Mediterranean or kalamata black olives (about 12)

A Dilly of a Vinaigrette (page 184) or other dressing

Bring 2 inches of water to a boil in a steamer pot or a stockpot with steamer basket. Add asparagus to steamer basket and cover. Reduce heat to simmer, and cook asparagus for 5 minutes. It should be bright green and crisp tender, not mushy (see notes below).

Place eggs in a small saucepan with enough water to cover. Bring to a boil over medium-high heat. Turn off heat and leave eggs in water for 20 minutes to hard cook. Drain water and cool eggs with cold running water. Give shells a tap to break, roll in hands to crack entire shell, and peel. Slice eggs with an egg slicer or knife.

To assemble salad: Place arugula on a platter. Layer top with tuna chunks, sliced eggs, asparagus, and olives, and drizzle with vinaigrette.

NOTES

If cooking the asparagus for an Explorer, remove the portion for the salad and continue to steam the asparagus until it becomes soft, in order to easily cut into bite-size pieces.

If making finger food for an Independent or older child, remove and serve the asparagus with Cheese Please! sauce (see page 120).

ASPARAGUS TIPS

Everyone likes the tips of the asparagus, but you don't need to waste the tender midsection or measure how much to trim off the bottom. To be sure you're removing the tough, woody end from the asparagus, simply hold the tip end in one hand and hold the bottom end between your other hand's thumb, index, and middle fingers. Now gently snap. The bottom will break off where it is tough.

NUTRITION FACTS

Serving Size: 1 cookie (18g)

Calories   50
Calories from Fat   0
Total Fat   0g
Saturated Fat   0g
Cholesterol   0mg
Sodium   10mg
Total Carbohydrate   13g
Dietary Fiber   less than 1g
Sugars   9g
Protein   1g

the
petit
appetit
COOKBOOK

♥

"Bran New" Macaroons

Here's a twist on the usual macaroon, with the addition of oat bran for the texture. This cookie is an especially good option for those allergic to nuts.

MAKES 12 TO 16 (2-INCH) COOKIES

1 cage-free, organic egg white
½ cup packed organic light brown sugar
¾ cup organic oat bran
½ teaspoon ground cinnamon

Preheat the oven to 350°F. Line a baking sheet with parchment paper.

In a large bowl, whisk the egg white until stiff peaks form. Whisk brown sugar into egg white. Sprinkle bran and cinnamon over egg mixture and gently fold together with a rubber spatula.

Drop teaspoons of dough on prepared baking sheet. You may need to use your fingers to push the dough together. Bake about 15 minutes, or until pale brown and beginning to crisp. Remove pan from oven and allow cookies to set on baking sheet for 1 to 2 minutes before transferring with a spatula to a wire rack to cool completely.

Baked Parsnips

Ron Siegel, chef of San Francisco's Masa's restaurant, told me in a cooking class to explore parsnips, as it was one of his children's favorites. He was right. Parsnips are often overlooked when shopping for vegetables, but their mild flavor and soft texture makes them appealing for small children.

MAKES 8 SERVINGS

4 medium organic parsnips (about 1 pound)
¼ cup olive oil
½ teaspoon sea salt
1 teaspoon minced fresh tarragon

Preheat oven to 400°F. Peel parsnips and cut into 1- to 2-inch chunks. Place in a self-sealing bag with olive oil. Seal bag and move parsnips around to coat with oil. Transfer parsnips to a glass baking dish in a single layer. Sprinkle salt and tarragon over parsnips. Bake about 40 minutes, stirring every 10 minutes to distribute herbs and oil. Parsnips are done when tender and golden.

CURIOUS ABOUT PRODUCE

Sometimes adults who were never introduced to certain varieties of produce never consider buying items such as parsnips for their family. Ask the farmer or grocer to identify an interesting new item and find out how best to cook and eat it. You may find a new favorite for you and your children.

NUTRITION FACTS

Serving Size: ⅛ of recipe (88g)

Calories 120
Calories from Fat 70
Total Fat 7g
Saturated Fat 1g
Cholesterol 0mg
Sodium 150mg
Total Carbohydrate 14g
Dietary Fiber 3g
Sugars 4g
Protein 1g

The Shakers:
Two to Three
Years

♥

Eggplant Rounds

How do you describe an eggplant to a child? It's not an egg and it's not a plant. It is, however, a member of the potato family and is known worldwide by names such as *aubergine*, *brinjal*, *melanzana*, *patlican*, and *garden egg*.

NUTRITION FACTS

Serving Size: ⅑ of recipe (85g)

Calories 50
Calories from Fat 15
Total Fat 2g
Saturated Fat 0.5g
Cholesterol 45mg
Sodium 70mg
Total Carbohydrate 6g
Dietary Fiber 2g
Sugars 3g
Protein 3g

MAKES 12 ROUNDS

1 medium (about 1 pound) organic eggplant
2 cage-free, organic eggs
¼ cup dry bread crumbs
¼ cup grated Parmesan cheese
Marinara sauce (page 148) or Happy Hummus (page 132), for dipping

Preheat oven to 425°F. Line a baking sheet with foil and spray lightly with olive oil. Cut eggplant crosswise into about ½-inch-thick rounds.

Lightly beat eggs in a shallow dish. Combine bread crumbs and cheese on a plate. Dip each eggplant round in eggs and then dredge each side in bread crumb mixture to coat. Place eggplant rounds on prepared baking sheet in a single layer. Bake for 15 to 20 minutes, turning once halfway through baking. Eggplant will turn golden and crumbs will crisp.

Serve with sauce for dipping.

TIP

How to choose an eggplant? Choose a firm, smooth-skinned eggplant that is heavy for its size. Gently push on the skin with your thumb or forefinger; if it springs back, it is ripe. If your finger indentation remains, it is mushy and thus overripe. If there is no give at all, the eggplant was picked too early and will be dry inside.

the
petit
appetit
COOKBOOK
♥

Fruit-Free Granola

I had a client who had a fruit allergy and couldn't find a fruit-free granola recipe for herself and toddler, Zuzu. I came up with this recipe, which does not contain any fruit or fruit juice. Of course, fruit lovers can add fresh or dried fruit to create a variety of textures and flavors.

MAKES ABOUT 8 CUPS

5 cups organic rolled oats

1 cup organic wheat germ

1 cup organic wheat bran

½ cup coarsely chopped raw almonds, walnuts, pecans, or combination

½ cup unsalted sunflower seeds

½ tablespoon ground cinnamon

½ cup maple syrup or pasteurized honey

⅓ cup expeller pressed canola oil

Preheat oven to 300°F. In a large bowl, stir together oats, germ, bran, nuts, seeds, and cinnamon. In a smaller bowl, whisk together syrup and oil. Stir syrup mixture into nut and grain mixture to coat and moisten.

Spread mixture evenly onto a greased jelly-roll pan. Bake for 30 to 35 minutes, or until lightly brown and crisp. Stir after 20 minutes of baking to be sure all sides are golden. Remove from oven and transfer with a spatula to parchment paper to cool. Break into desired size clusters and enjoy dry as a snack, or with milk, yogurt, or cottage cheese.

TIP

Eat some now, save some for later! Store the granola in an airtight container for up to 2 weeks at room temperature. For longer storage, seal in freezer bags and place in the freezer for up to 2 months.

NUTRITION FACTS

Serving Size: ½ cup (60g)

Calories 250
Calories from Fat 100
Total Fat 11g
Saturated Fat 1g
Cholesterol 0mg
Sodium 0mg
Total Carbohydrate 33g
Dietary Fiber 6g
Sugars 9g
Protein 9g

The Shakers:
Two to Three
Years

♥

Gabby's Gazpacho

Three-year-old Gabby called this soup "punch" because, she said, "it couldn't be soup, since soup was hot." I think it's a good way to give your family a powerful "punch" of vegetables full of folic acid and fiber. It's a refreshing meal on a hot summer day.

MAKES ABOUT 6 CUPS

5 medium vine-ripened organic tomatoes, quartered (about 4½ cups)

½ medium organic cucumber, peeled and sliced (about 1 cup)

½ cup cooked or canned garbanzo beans

⅛ cup chopped organic red onion

2 tablespoons chopped fresh basil

1 teaspoon salt

½ cup vegetable broth

¼ cup olive oil

2 tablespoons balsamic vinegar

GARNISH (OPTIONAL)

½ cup chopped avocado, tomato, and/or peeled cucumber

Blend all ingredients except optional garnish in a food processor or blender until smooth, 2 to 3 minutes. Transfer to a container and chill in the refrigerator for 1 hour. Ladle into soup bowls and top with garnish, if desired.

the
petit
appetit
COOKBOOK
♥

Honey-Mustard Baked Chicken

This is a very quick recipe for busy families. Simply make the marinade in the morning (or the night before) and bake when you're ready. You'll save on time and cleanup because you marinate and bake the chicken in a single dish.

For an easy meal serve this chicken over polenta or couscous.

MAKES 4 SERVINGS

4 boneless, skinless organic chicken breast halves (about 2 pounds)
¼ cup pasteurized honey
¼ cup Dijon mustard
1½ teaspoons curry powder
1 tablespoon naturally brewed soy sauce (tamari)

Place chicken snugly in a single layer in a baking dish. Whisk together honey, mustard, curry powder, and soy sauce in a small bowl. Pour marinade over chicken; cover, and refrigerate for 6 hours or overnight. Turn once or twice to coat chicken with marinade.

When ready to cook, preheat oven to 350°F. Cover chicken with foil and bake for 1 hour. Remove cover, baste, and turn chicken over. Bake an additional 15 minutes. Transfer chicken to a platter and spoon sauce over to serve.

EGG FREE

GLUTEN FREE

NUTRITION FACTS

Serving Size: 1 piece (127g)

Calories 230
Calories from Fat 30
Total Fat 3g
Saturated Fat 1g
Cholesterol 75mg
Sodium 650mg
Total Carbohydrate 21g
Dietary Fiber 0g
Sugars 17g
Protein 30g

The Shakers:
Two to Three
Years

♥

the
petit
appetit
COOKBOOK
♥

Hula Smoothie

On a hot day, make this cool smoothie and pretend you and your child are on a tropical island. All you need now is a grass skirt.

MAKES ABOUT 3 CUPS

1 cup organic strawberries

1 medium organic banana, frozen

½ cup organic vanilla yogurt

1 cup organic pineapple juice

Combine all ingredients in a blender and process until smooth.

YEAH YOGURT!

Your growing baby needs saturated fat and cholesterol for the normal development of the brain and nervous system. Yogurt is a good way to deliver fat, protein, and calcium for: brain development; growth and maintenance of muscle, bone, and cartilage; teeth; and every system in your child's body.

Presto Pizza Dough

There's no other kitchen activity that's more fun for kids than creating their own personal pizzas. Kids love to knead dough and choose their own toppings. It is not necessary to have perfect pies, so get your hands in there instead of using a rolling pin. This dough makes pizza, breadsticks, and teething biscuits.

MAKES 1 (12- TO 14-INCH) PIZZA OR 12 BREADSTICKS

1 package (1 tablespoon) yeast
½ cup plus 2 tablespoons warm water
¾ cups organic whole wheat flour
¾ cups unbleached all-purpose flour
¼ cup olive oil
½ teaspoon salt

In a large bowl, dissolve yeast in warm water; let stand until foamy. Add remaining ingredients to yeast and water. Mix together and knead by hand until dough is smooth, about 3 minutes. Make dough into a ball, return to bowl, and cover with plastic wrap. Let rise until doubled, about 30 minutes.

For pizza: Place dough on a greased baking or pizza pan and press with your fingers to spread to cover pan bottom. Add desired sauce and toppings and bake in a preheated 425°F oven for 15 to 20 minutes, or until crust is brown on the edges.

For bread sticks: Divide dough into 12 portions and roll with hands into stick shapes of desired width, fatter for soft breadsticks and thinner for hard. Place sticks on a greased baking pan and bake in a preheated 425°F oven for 8 to 10 minutes, or until edges are golden.

For teething biscuits: Make into breadsticks. Place breadsticks in freezer to harden for a cool, soothing treat. Be sure to carefully monitor baby while chewing on the frozen breadsticks.

NUTRITION FACTS

Serving Size: 1 breadstick or ¹⁄12 pizza dough without toppings (26g)

Calories 70
Calories from Fat 0
Total Fat 0g
Saturated Fat 0g
Cholesterol 0mg
Sodium 100mg
Total Carbohydrate 13g
Dietary Fiber 2g
Sugars 0g
Protein 3g

The Shakers:
Two to Three
Years

♥

Double time. You can double the ingredients to make one thick-crust pizza or two thin-crust pizzas. Make one thin-crust pizza now and save the second dough ball in the freezer for the next time your little ones ask for pizza.

Rosemary Castle Potatoes

I call these castle potatoes, because while traveling with my mom in England we had dinner in a castle that served these wonderful potatoes. I came home and was inspired to re-create the dinner and remind me of the trip.

MAKES 6 SERVINGS

2 pounds small organic white new or fingerling potatoes (about 24), scrubbed

¼ cup olive oil

1 tablespoon chopped fresh rosemary

½ teaspoon coarse sea salt

Preheat oven to 425°F. Line a 9 × 13-inch baking pan with foil. Cut potatoes in half and place in a plastic self-sealing bag. Pour olive oil over potatoes and move bag to coat potatoes. Transfer potatoes to prepared pan. Bruise rosemary with back of a spoon or mortar and pestle to release oil. Sprinkle salt and rosemary over potatoes and stir to mix. Bake for 35 to 45 minutes, or until potatoes are brown on the outside and tender inside.

POTATO FACTS

The United States produces about 35 billion pounds of potatoes annually. Americans consume about 126 pounds per person per year, on average—far more than any other vegetable. Unfortunately, 65 percent of the potatoes consumed are not sold fresh, but in convenient forms, such as french fries, which add sodium and fat to Americans' diets as well.

NUTRITION FACTS

Serving Size: 1 cup (161g)

Calories 190
Calories from Fat 90
Total Fat 10g
Saturated Fat 1.5g
Cholesterol 0mg
Sodium 200mg
Total Carbohydrate 24g
Dietary Fiber 4g
Sugars 2g
Protein 3g

The Shakers:
Two to Three
Years

♥

EGG
FREE

Sloppy Janes

Joe is always getting blamed for sloppiness. Little girls can be pretty messy, too, so I've dedicated this to them. This recipe makes great use of the Tangy Barbecue Sauce on page 167; however, feel free to substitute with your family's favorite sauce for a quick variation.

MAKES 6 SERVINGS

1 small organic yellow onion, chopped (about ½ cup)

½ large green bell pepper, chopped (about ½ cup)

1 cup (6 ounces) organic mushrooms, chopped

1 pound organic ground beef round

2 cups Tangy Barbecue Sauce (page 167) or prepared sauce

½ teaspoon salt

⅛ teaspoon black pepper

½ teaspoon minced fresh oregano

½ teaspoon minced fresh thyme

6 rolls, split and toasted

Heat a large nonstick skillet over medium heat. Add onion, bell pepper, mushrooms, and beef. Cook, stirring to break up beef, until vegetables are soft and beef is browned. Stir in barbecue sauce and remaining ingredients. Reduce heat to medium-low, cover, and cook until heated throughout, about 15 minutes

Spoon ½ cup of the beef mixture on each roll. Eat open-faced or as a sandwich.

NUTRITION FACTS

Serving Size: 1 sandwich (378g)

Calories 420
Calories from Fat 130
Total Fat 15g
Saturated Fat 5g
Cholesterol 60mg
Sodium 480mg
Total Carbohydrate 50g
Dietary Fiber 8g
Sugars 14g
Protein 25g

the
petit
appetit
COOKBOOK
♥

Soba Stir-Fry

Soba noodles are Japanese noodles made of buckwheat flour (*soba-ko*) and wheat flour (*komugi-ko*). They are roughly as thick as spaghetti and prepared in various hot and cold dishes. Children are impressed by the simple yet elegant-looking vegetable ribbons that complete this stir-fry.

MAKES 2 SERVINGS

1 tablespoon expeller pressed canola oil

1 teaspoon grated orange zest

2 teaspoons grated ginger (about 1-inch piece)

1 large garlic glove, minced

1 medium organic zucchini, peeled into ribbons

1 medium organic carrot, peeled into ribbons

½ cup fresh organic soybeans (edamame)

1 cup (6 ounces) sliced organic mushrooms (crimini, shiitake, or combination)

SAUCE

2 tablespoons natural low-sodium soy sauce (tamari)

1 teaspoon pasteurized honey

5 ounces uncooked soba noodles

¼ cup chopped scallions (optional)

Heat oil in large skillet or wok over medium-high heat. Add zest, ginger, and garlic and stir-fry quickly so garlic does not burn. When spices are fragrant, add zucchini, carrot, soybeans, and mushrooms to skillet. Stir-fry about 3 minutes, or until heated through.

To make sauce: Whisk together soy sauce and honey in a small bowl.

Heat water in a saucepan until boiling. Add soba noodles and cook until tender, 5 minutes. Drain noodles in a colander. Add noodles and sauce to vegetables and toss to combine.

NUTRITION FACTS

Serving Size: 1 cup (240g)

Calories 380
Calories from Fat 150
Total Fat 17g
Saturated Fat 2g
Cholesterol 0mg
Sodium 600mg
Total Carbohydrate 40g
Dietary Fiber 7g
Sugars 5g

The Shakers:
Two to Three
Years

♥

SIMPLE SOBA

The most basic soba dish is zaru, in which boiled, cold soba noodles are eaten with a simple soy dipping sauce.

Spanish Rice

This recipe makes slightly spicy rice that is very versatile. For vegans and vegetarians it can be enjoyed as a side dish with black beans or wrapped in a vegetable burrito. Those who eat meat can transform this rice into a festive meal by adding chunks of chicken, meat, or seafood. Paella anyone?

MAKES 4 SERVINGS

2 teaspoons olive oil

1 large shallot, chopped (about ¼ cup)

¼ cup organic carrot, chopped

½ cup organic tomatoes, chopped

⅛ teaspoon cayenne pepper

1 teaspoon ground cumin

1 cup uncooked organic brown rice

2 cups organic vegetable broth

½ teaspoon salt

Heat olive oil in large stockpot over low heat. Add shallot, carrot, and tomatoes and sauté until shallot is translucent, for 3 minutes. Add spices, rice, broth, and salt. Cover and bring to a boil, then reduce heat and simmer until rice is tender, about 45 minutes. Check every 10 minutes to be sure the broth has not all been absorbed too quickly; add more liquid if needed.

NUTRITION FACTS

Serving Size: 1 cup (191g)

Calories 230
Calories from Fat 35
Total Fat 4g
Saturated Fat 0.5g
Cholesterol 0mg
Sodium 640mg
Total Carbohydrate 44g
Dietary Fiber 3g
Sugars 4g
Protein 5g

The Shakers:
Two to Three
Years

♥

NUTRITION FACTS

Serving Size: 1 waffle (110g)

Calories 270
Calories from Fat 150
Total Fat 17g
Saturated Fat 2g
Cholesterol 55mg
Sodium 300mg
Total Carbohydrate 24g
Dietary Fiber 3g
Sugars 0g
Protein 7g

the
petit
appetit
COOKBOOK

♥

Three-Grain Waffles

These make an easy, healthy breakfast for the whole family. More than a few families make waffles and pancakes as a family ritual every weekend. To keep cooked waffles warm while baking remaining batches, place waffles on a baking rack atop a cookie sheet and place it in a 300°F oven.

MAKES 8 WAFFLES

¾ cup organic whole-wheat flour

½ cup organic buckwheat flour

½ cup organic rice flour

1 tablespoon baking powder

¼ teaspoon salt

¼ teaspoon ground nutmeg

2 cage-free, organic eggs

1¾ cups organic milk

½ cup expeller pressed canola oil

In a mixing bowl, combine flours, baking powder, salt, and nutmeg. In a smaller bowl, beat eggs slightly. Beat milk and oil into eggs. Add egg mixture to flour mixture all at once and beat until just combined. The batter will be lumpy.

Pour 1 to 1¼ cups of batter onto grid of preheated waffle maker. Close lid quickly. Cook according to manufacturer's directions. Do not lift lid until baking time is complete. When cooked, use a fork or tongs to remove waffle. Repeat with remaining batter.

TIP

Creating convenience. Make extra waffles and freeze in freezer bags. You can create your own toaster waffles for breakfasts or snacks. See page 249 for more ways to enjoy waffles.

Toasted Pilaf

Unlike a typical rice pilaf, this recipe is lighter and sweeter. The toasting brings out a richer, nuttier flavor. This makes a great accompaniment or stuffing for meats, fish, or vegetables.

MAKES 3 CUPS

½ cup organic quinoa

½ cup organic buckwheat

⅛ teaspoon curry powder

⅛ teaspoon ground cumin

2 cups organic vegetable broth

Toast the grains in a large saucepan over low heat, stirring constantly, until quinoa looks golden and aromatic, about 1 minute. Stir in curry powder and cumin. Remove pan from heat and let cool for 5 minutes. Add the vegetable broth and bring to a boil over medium-high heat. Reduce heat, cover, and simmer about 25 minutes. Check every 10 minutes to be sure the broth has not all been absorbed too quickly; add more liquid if needed. Pilaf is done when grains are tender and liquid is absorbed. Fluff with a fork.

TIP
Great grains. Feel free to experiment with single grains or a combination for this recipe. This can be made with amaranth, millet, or even brown rice. If you use rice, you'll need to increase the cooking time.

NUTRITION FACTS
Serving Size: 1 cup (216g)

Calories 220
Calories from Fat 25
Total Fat 2.5g
Saturated Fat 0g
Cholesterol 0mg
Sodium 320mg
Total Carbohydrate 43g
Dietary Fiber 5g
Sugars 2g
Protein 8g

The Shakers:
Two to Three
Years

♥

Tuna Stuffing

Many children like tuna sandwiches but are not fans of mayonnaise. This recipe is different, as it is lighter in texture but richer in flavor, because it uses lemon juice in place of mayonnaise.

MAKES 2 SERVINGS

1 (6.5-ounce) can water-packed white or chunk light albacore tuna

1 teaspoon capers, chopped

1 tablespoon freshly squeezed lemon juice

1 teaspoon chopped fresh dill

1 teaspoon finely chopped scallion (optional)

Drain tuna and flake with a fork into a medium bowl. Add remaining ingredients and mix with a fork. Store in an airtight container in the refrigerator for up to 2 days.

Serve tuna stuffed into pita bread, rolled in lettuce leaves, or as a dip with crackers and vegetable sticks.

TIP

Stuff it! This tuna stuffing is a good option when packing your child's lunch for travel or a picnic. Because the tuna is not dripping with mayonnaise, the sandwich will not be soggy waiting for lunchtime. Remember to use an ice pack or cooler bag to keep it cold.

the
petit
appetit
COOKBOOK
♥

Chestnut-Squash Sauté

This is a unique and festive side dish for the holiday table. Acorn squash look like giant acorns and come in orange, green, or yellow. All are good choices for this recipe.

MAKES 3 SERVINGS

1 medium (about 8-ounce) organic acorn squash

⅓ cup chopped roasted chestnuts (6 to 8 nuts [see roasting recipe on page 233])

1 tablespoon unsalted butter

1 tablespoon olive oil

½ teaspoon minced fresh thyme

Sea salt and pepper, to taste

Preheat oven to 375°F. Cut squash in half lengthwise and scoop out seeds with a spoon. Place halves cut side down in a baking pan lined with aluminum foil. Bake about 30 minutes, or until flesh is fork tender. Remove flesh from peel and cut into 1½- to 2-inch cubes.

Melt butter in a saucepan over medium heat. Add oil and heat until shimmering. Add squash pieces, chestnuts, and spices and stir with a wooden spoon. Sauté over medium heat until squash is golden, butter is absorbed into squash, and everything is heated throughout.

TIP

Time is on your side. Often the holiday side dishes are overlooked since the focus is on the main dish already cooking in the oven. If you don't have the oven space or need to make this dish quickly, steam the squash in the microwave on High for 6 to 7 minutes and skip the oven.

NUTRITION FACTS

Serving Size: about 4 oz (93g)

Calories 130
Calories from Fat 60
Total Fat 7g
Saturated Fat 2.5g
Cholesterol 10mg
Sodium 75mg
Total Carbohydrate 18g
Dietary Fiber 4g
Sugars 2g
Protein 1g

The Shakers:
Two to Three
Years

♥

Cranberry Sauce

Everyone loves cranberry sauce for the holidays. This has just the right balance of sweet and tart and makes a great spread for turkey, beef, or veggie sandwiches anytime of the year. Just remember to freeze some cranberries during the winter to enjoy when they are out of season.

MAKES ABOUT 1 CUP

1 cup fresh cranberries

¼ cup organic apple juice

¼ cup raw sugar

½ teaspoon ground cinnamon

¼ teaspoon grated lemon zest

Combine all ingredients in a saucepot, and cook over medium heat. As mixture heats, cranberries will make a popping sound as skins break open. Sauce is ready when cranberries have popped and sauce is thick, 5 to 8 minutes.

CAUTION WITH CRANBERRIES

When cranberries get hot and their skins start to break open, they often spit juice. Be careful when stirring and don't cook cranberries over too high a heat.

---

the
petit
appetit
COOKBOOK
♥

Chapter 12

The Connoisseurs: Three to Four Years

Introduction Map

(Can eat all Shakers' food, plus the following)

FOODS APPROPRIATE	REASON	CONSISTENCY/TEXTURE
Liquids: lower fat cow's milk, water, soy and rice beverages, juice	After age two, children can have lower fat versions of dairy products	Anything and everything!
Nuts, shellfish, and any other foods that were avoided due to allergen risks	Now have enzymes to digest foods previously avoided. May have grown out of allergy; consult doctor before reintroducing.	Child will self-feed, but may need assistance cutting.

READY?

By this time the child may prefer Neiman Schell beef to McDonald's, or not. Moderation is key. Children will be influenced by forces outside your control, such as school and television. Balance your children's television watching (complete with fast-food advertising and jingles) with positive culinary learning experiences, such as trips to a farm or a fine dining restaurant. Hopefully the efforts you've made along your child's culinary adventure will lead them to healthy food choices and habits that will last a lifetime.

SET?

Get them involved with tasks for their age and stage. Ask for their help and opinions for mealtimes. Show them respect at the dinner table, just as you expect theirs in return. See more tips about getting your child involved in Chapter 4, Parenting in the Kitchen. Ask them to help plan menus and get their creative juices going. Branch out with unique spices and ingredients in ethnic recipes. Extend the learning to geography and anthropology by choosing a country, culture, or heritage and preparing a meal to fit the lesson. Pretend you're having dinner in India or breakfast in Japan.

GO!

Be patient. Rushing through a recipe is easy to do on your own, but demonstrating the process to a child will take time. Keep your promises. If you told them they can help, go at their pace and have fun.

Don't be surprised if your connoisseur also becomes a food critic. They may appreciate good food and expect high quality. "Children have to learn to dine and know how to behave at the dinner table. So the best thing is to take them out," says a mother and Culinary Institute of America graduate. "I did that with my daughter and created a true fine diner. At five years old she sent back her clams linguine because she ordered the red sauce and the waiter brought white."

The children are now older, so you may have more time and energy to spend in the kitchen if you're interested. Choose your family's own holiday traditions and food items to prepare for your extended family and friends. This chapter will help you discover family meals for every day and every age, from reinventing weeknight leftovers, to Sunday suppers entertaining friends. You'll also find recipes to involve your child in the cooking process and festive foods to celebrate milestones and holidays.

The Connoisseurs: Recipes

Oatmeal Cookies

These are a favorite with adults and kids alike. Three-year-old Jeffrey's mom called these "morning cookies," because her son insisted he didn't like oatmeal, but loved these cookies. She would have to measure the oats secretly, when he wasn't watching.

MAKES ABOUT 20 COOKIES

½ cup unsalted butter

⅔ cup packed organic light brown sugar

1 cage-free, organic egg

1 teaspoon vanilla extract

½ cup unbleached all-purpose flour

½ cup organic whole-wheat flour

½ teaspoon baking soda

¼ teaspoon salt

¼ teaspoon ground cinnamon

1 cup old-fashioned rolled organic oats

½ cup organic golden raisins

½ cup dried cranberries

Preheat oven to 350°F. Line baking sheets with parchment paper. Cream butter and sugar together in a large bowl until light and fluffy. Add egg and vanilla and beat well. Stir together flours, baking soda, salt, and cinnamon in a medium bowl. Fold dry ingredients into butter mixture until dough comes together. Stir in oats and raisins until just combined.

Drop dough by tablespoons onto prepared baking sheets. Bake for 10 to 12 minutes, or until golden brown. Let cookies set on baking sheet for 2 minutes, then transfer with a spatula to a wire rack to cool completely.

NUTRITION FACTS

Serving Size: 1 cookie (28g)

Calories 110
Calories from Fat 45
Total Fat 5g
Saturated Fat 3g
Cholesterol 20mg
Sodium 40mg
Total Carbohydrate 17g
Dietary Fiber less than 1g
Sugars 11g
Protein 1g

Southwestern Salad Vinaigrette

This recipe was adapted from Saint Louis Art Museum's cookbook *The Artist in the Kitchen*. Appropriately, this salad is so colorful you will think it is a work of art. Be sure to show off its colors in a glass bowl. It is a wonderful addition to any picnic or summer barbecue.

MAKES 6 SERVINGS

2 cups cooked or canned organic black beans, rinsed

2 large organic red pepper, diced (about 2 cups)

1 large organic green pepper, diced (about 1 cup)

2 cups organic cooked corn kernels

¼ cup sherry wine vinegar

1 tablespoon Dijon mustard

1 tablespoon ground cumin

1 teaspoon salt

1 teaspoon black pepper

¼ cup expeller pressed canola oil

½ pint organic cherry tomatoes, cut in half

¼ cup diced organic green onions

In a large glass bowl, combine beans, bell peppers, and corn. In a small bowl, whisk together vinegar, mustard, cumin, salt, pepper, and oil. Pour dressing over bean mixture and toss well to combine. Add tomatoes and green onions and lightly toss just before serving.

TIP

Do the cancan. If using canned beans, be sure to rinse thoroughly to remove some of the sodium used in the canning process.

the
petit
appetit
COOKBOOK
♥

Popped Corn

Most kids don't have any idea that popcorn really is corn. In the seventies and eighties popcorn came from a silver foil bag or an air-popper appliance. Now most children think popcorn only comes from the microwave. If you have a pot with a clear lid, you and your child will enjoy witnessing the "pop."

MAKES 7 TO 8 CUPS

2 tablespoons peanut oil

⅓ cup unpopped popcorn

Put oil and one kernel of popcorn in a large heavy-bottom pot. Cover and heat over medium-high heat. When the kernel pops, about 3 minutes, add the remaining popcorn in a single layer and cover. Once pops are less frequent, move pan a few times back and forth over heat, until pops stop. Remove pot from heat, carefully remove lid, and transfer popcorn to a large bowl.

TIP

Top on pop. Add a sprinkling of desired topping. Or make separate bowls for each family member to dress and enjoy his own creation. Some suggestions include cinnamon, cayenne pepper, Parmesan cheese (sorry vegans), paprika, salt, pepper, and sugar.

NUTRITION FACTS

Serving Size: 2 cups (23g)

Calories 120
Calories from Fat 70
Total Fat 8g
Saturated Fat 1g
Cholesterol 0mg
Sodium 0mg
Total Carbohydrate 12g
Dietary Fiber 2g
Sugars 0g
Protein 2g

The
Connoisseurs:
Three to Four
Years

♥

Portobello Burgers

Portobello mushrooms are often referred to as "the steaks of the mushroom family." This is a creative way to enjoy a burger without the meat. Just like other burgers, you can even cook them outdoors.

MAKES 4 SERVINGS

4 large portobello mushrooms

2 tablespoons olive oil

2 tablespoons balsamic vinegar

1 tablespoon fresh dill, thyme, or oregano

¼ teaspoon pepper

¼ teaspoon salt

TO SERVE (OPTIONAL)

1 large French or sourdough baguette

Swiss cheese slices

Dijon mustard

Arugula leaves

Remove stems from mushrooms and place caps in a single layer in a glass dish. Whisk olive oil, vinegar, dill, pepper, and salt in a small bowl until combined. Pour oil and vinegar mixture over mushrooms and turn to coat both sides. Let sit for 20 to 30 minutes.

Heat a large skillet or grill pan over medium-high heat. When hot, add mushrooms and cook 2 to 3 minutes on each side, turning with a spatula. Mushrooms will be soft and turn dark when cooked.

To serve (if using): Cut baguette in four equal portions and slice in half lengthwise. Place mushrooms on baguette and top with cheese, mustard, and arugula. Or serve with your own family's favorite toppings.

TIP

To clean mushrooms, gently wipe with a damp cloth or soft mushroom brush. If you need to rinse them, do not do so until you are ready to use them; use cold water and pat dry with paper towel.

NUTRITION FACTS

Serving Size: 1 burger without bread or topping (145g)

Calories 250
Calories from Fat 140
Total Fat 16g
Saturated Fat 6g
Cholesterol 25mg
Sodium 380mg
Total Carbohydrate 15g
Dietary Fiber 2g
Sugars 3g
Protein 12g

the
petit
appetit
COOKBOOK
♥

Easter Bread

Many cultures make breads to mark the Easter season and give as gifts to friends and family. Whether it's a Polish *babka*, a Russian *kulich*, or an Italian *pan di pasqua*, this beautiful, egg-based bread would be welcome on any Easter brunch or dinner table. Variations include adding nuts, dried fruits, and even a whole colored Easter egg.

MAKES 20 SERVINGS; 2 LOAVES

4 ½ cups unbleached all-purpose flour

¼ cup organic cane sugar

1 teaspoon salt

2 packages (about 2 tablespoons) quick-rising yeast

½ cup milk

½ cup water

2 tablespoons unsalted butter

3 cage-free, organic eggs, at room temperature

EGG WASH

1 cage-free, organic egg yolk

1 tablespoon cold milk

Sesame seeds (optional)

In large bowl, combine 3½ cups of the flour, sugar, salt, and yeast. In a small saucepan, heat milk, water, and butter until hot to touch, but not boiling. Stir milk mixture into flour mixture; dough will be crumbly. Mix in eggs with a stand or handheld mixer and slowly beat in remaining flour by tablespoonfuls. Use only enough remaining flour to make dough soft and not sticky. Turn out dough onto floured surface, and knead until soft and elastic, about 4 minutes.

Preheat oven to 400°F. Divide dough into six equal pieces; roll each into a 12-inch rope. Braid three ropes together; seal ends. Repeat with remaining ropes. Place on greased baking sheets; let dough rise for 15 to 20 minutes.

To make egg wash: Beat egg yolk with milk. Brush egg wash on bread loaves, and then sprinkle with sesame seeds, if desired. Bake

NUTRITION FACTS

Serving Size: 1 slice (55g)

Calories 150
Calories from Fat 25
Total Fat 2.5g
Saturated Fat 1g
Cholesterol 45mg
Sodium 135mg
Total Carbohydrate 25g
Dietary Fiber 1g
Sugars 3g
Protein 5g

The Connoisseurs: Three to Four Years

♥

loaves for 20 minutes, or until brown on tops and hollow when thumped on the bottoms. Remove from baking sheet, and cool on wire racks.

TIP

Two for one. This recipe is great because you can enjoy one loaf now and freeze one for later. Or better yet, give one away and keep one for your family.

Black Bean Soup

Some like it hot! Adjust the chiles in this recipe to suit your family's taste buds. Start with a recipe of your baby's pureed black beans (page 95) and take it from there.

MAKES 6 SERVINGS

1 cup pureed black beans (page 95), coarsely pureed

4 cups vegetable broth

2 tablespoons olive oil

3 large garlic cloves, minced

1 small onion, diced (about ½ cup)

1 medium red bell pepper, diced (about 1 cup)

1 large Anaheim chile, stemmed, seeded, and chopped

1 jalapeo or serrano chile, stemmed, seeded, and chopped

½ cup chopped fresh cilantro leaves

In a large pot, combine bean puree and broth. Heat oil in a skillet over medium heat. Add garlic, onion, bell pepper, and chiles and sauté until vegetables are softened and onion is translucent, about 6 minutes.

Stir sautéed vegetables into bean mixture and simmer over medium heat for about 20 minutes. Stir in cilantro and cook until flavors are combined and heated through, about 3 minutes.

ANCIENT BEANS

The common black or turtle bean is thought to have originated in southern Mexico and Central America more than 7,000 years ago. Evidence of its use has been found in excavations of prehistoric dwellings.

NUTRITION FACTS

Serving Size: 1 cup (225g)

Calories 110
Calories from Fat 45
Total Fat 5g
Saturated Fat 0.5g
Cholesterol 0mg
Sodium 600mg
Total Carbohydrate 15g
Dietary Fiber 3g
Sugars 4g
Protein 3g

The
Connoisseurs:
Three to Four
Years

♥

Vegan Carob-Banana Cookies

This cookie looks just like a gooey chocolate chip cookie, but made especially for vegans without the butter, eggs, and chocolate.

MAKES 30 (2-INCH) COOKIES

¾ cup unbleached all-purpose flour

1 cup organic rolled oats

1½ teaspoons organic ground cinnamon

½ teaspoon baking soda

2 tablespoons organic soy flour

1 tablespoon water

2 medium bananas, mashed (about 1 cup)

2 tablespoons organic light brown sugar

2 teaspoons grated orange zest

1 teaspoon organic vanilla extract

½ cup vegan carob chips

Preheat oven to 350°F. Line 2 baking sheets with parchment paper. In a large mixing bowl, combine all-purpose flour, oats, cinnamon, and baking soda and whisk until well blended. In a small bowl, whisk together soy flour and water. In a food processor or blender, combine bananas, soy flour mixture, brown sugar, zest, and vanilla until smooth and creamy.

Fold banana mixture into oat mixture. Fold in carob chips. Drop dough by rounded tablespoons onto prepared baking sheets. Bake for about 10 minutes, or until golden brown on bottoms. Remove pans from oven and transfer cookies with a spatula to wire racks to cool completely.

AN EGG-CELLENT REPLACEMENT

Combine 1 tablespoon soy flour with 2 tablespoons of water to replace a single egg in a recipe.

NUTRITION FACTS

Serving Size: 1 cookie (23g)

Calories 50
Calories from Fat 10
Total Fat 1g
Saturated Fat 1g
Cholesterol 0mg
Sodium 25mg
Total Carbohydrate 10g
Dietary Fiber less than 1g
Sugars 4g
Protein 1g

the
petit
appetit
COOKBOOK
♥

Pork Roast with Blackberry Sauce

Pork loin has the great taste of pork chops and the impressive appearance of a roast, which makes it an easy option for a large family or group of friends. Serve with Rosemary Castle Potatoes (page 199) or Toasted Pilaf (page 205). The blackberry sauce gives this roast a sweet crust that children and adults love.

MAKES 10 SERVINGS

1 (2-pound) organic pork loin roast
⅔ cup organic blackberry all-fruit spread
1 tablespoon balsamic vinegar

Preheat oven to 375°F. Line a roasting pan with foil, and set a greased metal rack on top. Place the roast on the rack. In a small saucepan, stir together fruit spread and vinegar and cook over medium-low heat until a thick sauce forms. Spoon half of sauce over roast to coat. Cook roast for 30 to 40 minutes per pound, or until meat thermometer reaches 145°F. Remove from oven, cover, and let stand 10 minutes before slicing.

When ready to eat, reheat remaining sauce over low heat until hot, and serve with roast.

TIP
Choose a lean roast from a trusted hormone-free purveyor, such as Niman Ranch.

EGG FREE

GLUTEN FREE

WHEAT FREE

NUTRITION FACTS

Serving Size: 4 ounces (113g)

Calories 280
Calories from Fat 120
Total Fat 13g
Saturated Fat 5g
Cholesterol 75mg
Sodium 55mg
Total Carbohydrate 14g
Dietary Fiber 0g
Sugars 13g
Protein 25g

The
Connoisseurs:
Three to Four
Years

♥

Bucking Brownies

These brownies get their name from the buckwheat flour, which is used instead of wheat flour. This recipe has fewer ingredients than most brownie recipes, because of the high-quality chocolate used. Bittersweet chocolate with a high content of cocoa solids (over 50 percent) gives the best flavor, without a need for added sugar.

MAKES 15 BROWNIES

12 ounces bittersweet Scharfenberger chocolate (70 percent solids), chopped into pieces

½ cup unsalted butter

½ cup buckwheat flour

2 large cage-free, organic eggs

½ teaspoon baking powder

Preheat oven to 350°F. Grease an 8-inch square baking dish with butter or oil. In a small saucepan over a larger pan of simmering water, melt chocolate and butter, stirring occasionally. With a rubber spatula, stir the flour, eggs, and baking powder into the chocolate mixture until combined and creamy. Pour chocolate mixture into prepared dish and bake for 30 to 35 minutes, until risen and just set to the touch. Remove from oven and allow to cool completely in dish before cutting or spooning.

REASON TO INDULGE

In case you needed another reason to make these brownies, dark chocolate (like tea and red wine) has been shown to promote healthy cholesterol levels and act as an antioxidant.

---

the
petit
appetit
COOKBOOK

Cinnamon Meringues

Who knew that three staple ingredients could make such a simple and elegant treat? These cookies are lighter than air, chewy on the inside, and crunchy on the out. They go great with coffee, tea, or milk.

MAKES ABOUT 40 (1½-INCH) COOKIES

3 cage-free, organic egg whites
½ cup packed light brown sugar
⅛ teaspoon ground cinnamon

Preheat oven to 275°F. Line 2 large baking sheets with parchment paper. Beat egg whites with a stand or hand mixer on high until they form stiff peaks. Whisk cinnamon and sugar, 1 tablespoon at a time, into egg whites. Mixture will be stiff and glossy. Drop dollops of meringue by tablespoons onto prepared baking. Bake for 40 minutes, and then turn off oven. Leave meringues in oven until cool, about 30 minutes.

TIP

Have meringue, will travel. These are a great option when you need to bring something for school sharing, bake sales, or mother's groups. Meringues won't weigh you down and travel easily without crumbling.

The
Connoisseurs:
Three to Four
Years

♥

Gingerbread Family

Gingerbread makes the perfect cookie (and activity) to do for the holidays. Your little ones will love to cut, roll, and decorate these cutouts. Add a name and decorate in a family member's likeness and these make fun place cards for festive gatherings.

NUTRITION FACTS

Serving Size: I gingerbread
(64g)

Calories 210
Calories from Fat 35
Total Fat 4g
Saturated Fat 2.5g
Cholesterol 10mg
Sodium 200mg
Total Carbohydrate 41g
Dietary Fiber 2g
Sugars 15g
Protein 4g

MAKES 12 TO 15 (5-INCH) COOKIES

¼ cup unsalted butter

½ cup lightly packed organic light brown sugar

½ cup mild molasses

1¾ cups unbleached all-purpose flour

1¾ cups organic whole-wheat flour

1 teaspoon baking soda

⅛ teaspoon freshly grated nutmeg

⅛ teaspoon ground cloves

½ teaspoon ground cinnamon

1 teaspoon ground ginger

½ teaspoon salt

⅓ cup water

Preheat oven to 350°F. Line 2 baking sheets with parchment paper. Beat butter and sugar in a large mixing bowl with a stand mixer. Add molasses and beat until well mixed. Stir together flours, baking soda, spices, and salt in a separate bowl. Alternately beat dry ingredients and water into butter mixture. Blend well after each addition. You may need to add a bit more water to bring the dough together. The dough will be thick and heavy; if a stand mixture is not available, finish mixing the dough by hand.

Roll out dough on lightly floured waxed paper or a nonstick mat. Cut gingerbread people or other favorite shapes with a floured cutter. Place cookie cutter on rolled dough and press down evenly. Pick up shapes with metal spatula to transfer to baking sheets. Continue to knead dough scraps to roll and cut more cookies. Decorate gingerbread people with currants for eyes, buttons, mouths, even belly buttons.

Bake cookies for 7 to 9 minutes, turning baking sheet 180 degrees, midway through baking. Check doneness by pressing on cookie. If the dough springs back, the cookies are done. Remove from oven and transfer to a wire rack to cool.

the
petit
appetit
COOKBOOK

♥

Herb Turkey Burgers

These are not the typical dried-out turkey burger. The addition of mushrooms and onions give this recipe a tender and juicy texture your family will love.

MAKES 8 SERVINGS

1 ½ pounds ground turkey

½ cup (3 ounces) minced mushrooms

½ small onion, minced (about ½ cup)

1 teaspoon prepared barbecue sauce

1 teaspoon chopped fresh oregano

1 teaspoon ground cumin

1 tablespoon balsamic vinegar

½ teaspoon Tabasco sauce

Cheese slices (optional)

TO SERVE (OPTIONAL)

Toasted buns, pita pockets, or your child's favorite bread

Spreads and condiments

In a medium bowl, combine all ingredients, except optional cheese, buns, and spreads, using a wooden spoon or your hands. Be sure mushrooms and onion are equally distributed throughout mixture. Using your hands, press meat together to form equal-sized patties.

Heat a grill pan or skillet over medium heat. Spray pan with cooking spray, and cook patties for 5 minutes. Flip patties and cook on other side for 5 minutes or until cooked through. If using a grill you will see grill marks. For cheeseburgers, remember to add a cheese slice to top of patty after flipping.

Place patties on buns, if desired. Here's where the kids can have a great time with individual spreads and condiments to personalize their burgers.

TIP

No bun required. Some kids would rather dip their patties right into ketchup or mustard and don't want a bun. You also will want to skip the bun if your family can't eat gluten or wheat products.

Chicken and Sausage Jambalaya

Jambalaya is an easy one-pot meal to make for the whole family. In the South this is considered a major comfort food. For a spicier meal, substitute a Cajun andouille sausage. This one is less spicy for little mouths and more health-conscious than authentic Jambalaya recipes. But there are plenty of flavors from all of the fresh ingredients. Serve with Citrus-Corn Muffins (page 99).

MAKES 6 SERVINGS

2 tablespoons expeller pressed canola oil

½ pound chicken-apple sausage, cut into ½-inch slices

1 small organic onion, chopped (about ½ cup)

1 large organic red bell pepper, chopped (about 1 cup)

1 clove garlic, minced

1¾ cups organic chicken broth

3 medium vine-ripened organic tomatoes, or 1 cup Pomi tomatoes, drained and chopped

¼ cup Pomi tomato sauce

1 bay leaf

½ teaspoon chopped fresh oregano

¼ teaspoon chili powder

½ teaspoon chili flakes

1 cup uncooked short-grain brown rice

1 large (¾ pound) boneless, skinless organic chicken breast, cut into 2-inch strips

Heat oil in a large, heavy stockpot over medium-high heat. Add sausage, onion, bell pepper, and garlic. Cook, stirring occasionally, until vegetables are tender, about 5 minutes. Stir in broth, tomatoes, tomato sauce, bay leaf, oregano, and spices. Bring to a boil. Reduce heat and simmer, uncovered, for 10 minutes, stirring occasionally. Stir in rice. Cover and simmer for 10 minutes, stirring occasionally. Add chicken, cover, and simmer until chicken is cooked and rice is tender, about 5 minutes. Let stand, covered, 10 minutes. Remove bay leaf before serving.

NUTRITION FACTS

Serving Size: 1 cup (306g)

Calories 390
Calories from Fat 130
Total Fat 15g
Saturated Fat 4.5g
Cholesterol 70mg
Sodium 220mg
Total Carbohydrate 34g
Dietary Fiber 2g
Sugars 5g
Protein 28g

The
Connoisseurs:
Three to Four
Years

♥

225

Lamb Stew

This is an aromatic Indian stew. It is best served over couscous or Toasted Pilaf (page 205). The sweet potato lends both a sweet and creamy texture your child will love.

MAKES 5 SERVINGS

1½ pounds boneless leg of lamb, cut into 1½-inch chunks

½ teaspoon salt

¼ teaspoon black pepper

1 tablespoon olive oil

1 medium onion, diced (about 1 cup)

¼ teaspoon ground cinnamon

¼ teaspoon fresh grated ginger

¼ teaspoon ground cumin

1 pound organic sweet potatoes, chopped (about 2 cups)

⅓ cup organic golden raisins

1 medium organic zucchini, cut into chunks (about ½ cup)

14 ounces organic chicken broth

Heat oven to 350°F. In a medium bowl, combine lamb, salt, and pepper. In a large Dutch oven, heat oil over high heat. Add lamb to pot and cook until browned, stirring occasionally. If pan is too crowded, brown lamb in batches. Add onion and spices to lamb and stir. Reduce heat to medium and cook until onion is soft, about 5 minutes. Stir in remaining ingredients and bring to a boil. Remove pan from heat and cover. Place in the oven to cook for 30 minutes, or until vegetables and lamb are tender.

TIP

Pull up a highchair. Baby can enjoy this stew, too. Puree some of the cooked stew in a food processor or blender.

NUTRITION FACTS

Serving Size: 1 cup (286g)

Calories 440
Calories from Fat 220
Total Fat 24g
Saturated Fat 10g
Cholesterol 130mg
Sodium 440mg
Total Carbohydrate 16g
Dietary Fiber 1g
Sugars 10g
Protein 38g

The
Connoisseurs:
Three to Four
Years

♥

Mediterranean Pasta

This pasta dish makes a quick and easy vegetarian dinner for the whole family. Feel free to substitute other vegetables and pasta shapes to make the most of what's in your refrigerator and pantry. Leftovers can be served cold, as a pasta salad at lunch or side salad for dinner.

MAKES 2 SERVINGS

8 ounces uncooked fusilli pasta

2 tablespoons olive oil

1 medium organic red bell pepper, chopped

1 cup 1-inch pieces organic broccolini or broccoli

⅓ cup kalamata olives, pitted and halved

½ cup organic cherry tomatoes, halved

¼ cup (2 ounces) crumbled feta cheese

Freshly ground sea salt and black pepper, to taste

Fill a large stockpot with water and add 1 teaspoon salt. Bring water to a boil over medium-high heat. Add pasta. While pasta is cooking, heat sauté pan over medium-high heat. Add 1 tablespoon of the olive oil. When oil is hot, add bell pepper, broccolini, and olives and sauté until soft, 3 to 4 minutes. Add tomatoes and heat for 1 minute. Test pasta for doneness. Drain pasta in a colander and return to stockpot. Add vegetables and remaining 1 tablespoon olive oil to pasta and toss. Add feta and stir gently to mix ingredients and melt cheese throughout. Season with salt and pepper.

PICK YOUR PASTA

Substitute your favorite pasta to suit your family's taste and diet. There are many options, including enriched egg noodles, no yolk, whole-wheat, durum semolina, quinoa pasta, and others. You can also vary the appearance and texture with different shapes. Choose from fusilli, rotelli, shells, bowties, macaroni, penne, pinwheels, and more. Get creative!

---

the
petit
appetit
COOKBOOK
♥

Poached Pears

Many poaching recipes use wine or liquor for the cooking liquid. However this one is child-friendly and alcohol-free. Poached fruit is an easy, but elegant dessert for a festive occasion. Serve pears alone or with poaching liquid, warm or chilled, spooned over ice cream, yogurt, or angle food cake.

MAKES 4 SERVINGS

4 medium organic pears (about 1¼ pounds), peeled, cored, and quartered

2 cups cranberry juice

2 cinnamon sticks

3 whole cloves

Zest of ½ orange, in strips

Put all ingredients into a large saucepan. Be sure the pan is not too large, so that the juice completely covers the pears. If the juice does not cover the pears and the fruit floats, place a small plate upside down in pot, to weight pears down in liquid. Bring to a simmer over medium heat and cook for 7 (for ripe fruit) to 10 minutes (for less ripe fruit). Pears should pierce easily with a fork.

To make syrup, transfer pears to a bowl. Simmer the poaching liquid until it is reduced by one-third and thickened to desired consistency, 30 to 40 minutes. Pears can be stored in poaching liquid in a covered container in the refrigerator for up to 3 days.

TAKE YOUR PICK FOR POACHING

This recipe works well with fruit of the same firmness and ripeness. You may even want to combine apples with pears. Softer fruit such as peaches and plums are also a good option, but you'll need to reduce the cooking time, so the fruit does not become mushy.

The Connoisseurs: Three to Four Years

♥

Quinoa-Stuffed Peppers

Quinoa is a super grain with a nutty flavor and light texture, similar to couscous. In this dish it complements the sweet peppers and savory spices and makes an exciting alternative to plain old rice stuffing. You can find quinoa in the bulk section of specialty and organic grocers.

MAKES 4 SERVINGS

½ cup organic quinoa

2 tablespoons olive oil

1½ cups water

½ teaspoon salt

½ teaspoon black pepper

½ teaspoon minced fresh basil

½ medium onion, chopped (about ½ cup)

2 small (4-ounce) organic zucchini, grated (1 cup)

2 tablespoons dried currants

1 tablespoon chopped fresh parsley

½ teaspoon ground cumin

2 tablespoons freshly squeezed lemon juice

4 large (6- to 8-ounce) red or yellow organic bell peppers

1 tablespoon dry bread crumbs

1 tablespoon grated Parmesan cheese

Preheat oven to 375°F. In a small saucepan, stir together quinoa and 1 tablespoon of the olive oil to coat. Add water, salt, pepper, and basil and bring to a boil over medium-high heat. Cover and simmer over low heat for 20 minutes. Quinoa will be translucent. Remove from heat.

Pour remaining 1 tablespoon olive oil into a large skillet and add onion, zucchini, currants, parsley, cumin, and lemon juice. Sauté over medium-high heat until onion is translucent, 3 to 5 minutes. Add quinoa to vegetable sauté and mix thoroughly until heated throughout.

Cut a circle around the stem of each pepper. Pull out top as well as any seeds and membranes inside. Trim base of peppers so they will stand upright in a pan and stuff generously with quinoa-vegetable mixture. Combine bread crumbs and cheese in a small bowl and sprin-

the
petit
appetit
COOKBOOK
♥

kle over stuffed peppers. Bake peppers for 25 minutes, or until peppers are cooked, cheese is melted, and crumbs are crisp.

KEEN FOR QUINOA

Quinoa is a valuable source of protein for vegetarian diets. Ounce for ounce it has as much protein as meat and it supplies more of the nutrients necessary for life than most other foods. It contains all the essential amino acids, the building blocks for protein, which makes it a unique and complete protein food.

NUTRITION FACTS

Serving Size: 1 cup (302g)

Calories   290
Calories from Fat   90
Total Fat   10g
Saturated Fat   2g
Cholesterol   5mg
Sodium   380mg
Total Carbohydrate   42g
Dietary Fiber   2g
Sugars   5g
Protein   9g

Ratatouille Pasta

Traditional ratatouille is a French recipe of stewed eggplant and tomatoes. This version adds a few other vegetables and serves as a chunky sauce for kids' favorite pasta.

MAKES 4 SERVINGS

½ medium organic eggplant, cut into 1-inch cubes (about 2 cups)

1 medium organic zucchini, cut into 1-inch cubes (about 1 cup)

1 cup (6 ounces) sliced organic mushrooms

1 medium organic red bell pepper, cut into 1-inch pieces (about 1 cup)

2 tablespoons olive oil

½ teaspoon salt

½ teaspoon black pepper

1 pound favorite pasta shape (penne, wagon wheels, rotelle)

SAUCE

½ cup Pomi chopped tomatoes

¼ cup balsamic vinegar

¼ cup grated Parmesan cheese

Preheat oven to 425°F. Line a large baking pan with foil. Toss vegetables, oil, salt, and pepper in prepared baking pan so vegetables are coated by oil. Bake for 10 to 12 minutes, or until vegetables are tender.

Cook pasta according to package directions in a large pot of salted boiling water until tender.

Combine sauce ingredients in a medium bowl. Drain pasta and return to cooking pot. Add vegetables and sauce to pasta and toss to combine.

RATATOUILLE PIZZA

What do children like better than pasta? Pizza! This sauce works great on top of pizza, too. See page 197 for pizza dough recipe.

Roasted Chestnuts

Chestnuts are an integral part of many holiday meals. As far back as I can remember, my mother, sister, and I would peel chestnuts on Thanksgiving morning to make my nana's chestnut stuffing recipe. Roasted chestnuts can be eaten as a snack or added to stuffing, salads, and soups.

MAKES 7 TO 8 SERVINGS

8 ounces chestnuts (16 to 18 nuts)

Preheat oven to 375°F. Place each nut flat side down on a cutting board. Hold individual nut firmly, between your thumb and forefinger. Using a paring knife, make a diagonal cut in the round side of the chestnut. Make a second diagonal cut in opposite direction so cut looks like two intersecting sides of a triangle.

Put chestnuts in a baking pan with ¼ cup water, so nuts do not burn. Nuts will not be covered by water. Bake for 10 to 12 minutes, or until cuts in shells widen. Test for doneness by peeling a nut. It is easiest to peel nuts when they are hot, but be careful of burning your fingers. Flesh should be soft inside.

NUTRITION FACTS

Serving Size: 2 chestnuts (30g)

Calories 70
Calories from Fat 5
Total Fat 0.5g
Saturated Fat 0g
Cholesterol 0mg
Sodium 0mg
Total Carbohydrate 16g
Dietary Fiber 2g
Sugars 3g
Protein 1g

The
Connoisseurs:
Three to Four
Years

Spinach Shrimpy Fusilli

Ask your child to say that ten times, fast. High in protein and iron, this dish is a good way to introduce shrimp into your family's diet. The pasta is creamy and comforting and really highlights the fresh flavor of the shrimp and spinach.

MAKES 4 SERVINGS

2 tablespoons unsalted butter

1 pound large shrimp, peeled and deveined

¼ teaspoon salt

8 ounces uncooked fusilli pasta

10 ounces fresh organic spinach leaves, torn into 2-inch pieces (about 2 cups)

¾ cup sliced organic pearl onions, about 8 to 10

1¼ cups organic vegetable broth

1 teaspoon finely grated lemon zest

⅓ cup whole-milk ricotta cheese

½ teaspoon freshly grated nutmeg

⅛ teaspoon freshly ground black pepper

Melt 1 tablespoon of the butter in a large nonstick skillet over medium-high heat. Add shrimp and salt and sauté until shrimp turn pink, 2 minutes. Remove shrimp from pan and set aside.

Cook pasta according to package directions in a large pot of salted boiling water until tender. Drain well and return hot pasta to cooking pot. Stir in spinach while pasta is hot and allow spinach to wilt.

Melt remaining 1 tablespoon butter in a skillet over medium heat, and add onion. Sauté, stirring often, until tender, 6 to 8 minutes. Stir in broth and lemon zest and cook until mixture begins to thicken slightly. Stir in ricotta cheese until combined. Stir in nutmeg and pepper. Add shrimp and ricotta mixture to pasta and gently toss together.

Stuffed Squash Boats

This recipe is the perfect mix of vegetables for a hearty family meal. Baking squash before stuffing brings out the sweetness by caramelizing some of its sugars.

MAKES 4 SERVINGS

- 2 (about 1-pound) organic acorn squash
- 2 tablespoons olive oil
- 1 large organic zucchini, cut into ¼-inch rounds (about 1 cup)
- 1 large organic yellow squash, cut into ¼-inch rounds (about 1 cup)
- ½ small organic yellow onion, chopped (about ½ cup)
- 1 cup (6 ounces) sliced organic mushrooms
- 1 medium organic tomato, cut into chunks (about ¾ cup)
- 1 tablespoon chopped fresh oregano
- ½ teaspoon salt
- ½ teaspoon freshly ground pepper
- ½ cup shredded mozzarella cheese

Preheat oven to 400°F. Cut squash in halves lengthwise. Scrape out membranes and seeds. Place halves cut side down in glass baking dish with ⅓ cup water. Bake for about 30 minutes, or until fork tender. Turn squash so cut side is up in baking dish.

While squash bakes, heat oil in a large skillet over medium heat. Add zucchini, yellow squash, and onion and sauté for about 5 minutes. Add mushrooms, tomato, oregano, salt, and pepper and sauté for 5 minutes, or until vegetables are tender, but not mushy.

Stuff each squash half with about ½ cup of sautéed vegetables. Sprinkle cheese over each stuffed squash. Bake about 10 minutes, or until cheese is melted and golden.

TIP
This squash looks like a large, dark green acorn. Clues to good quality are a smooth, dry skin, free of cracks or soft spots.

NUTRITION FACTS

Serving Size: ½ stuffed squash (410g)

Calories 240
Calories from Fat 90
Total Fat 10g
Saturated Fat 2.5g
Cholesterol 10mg
Sodium 390mg
Total Carbohydrate 35g
Dietary Fiber 6g
Sugars 9g
Protein 8g

The Connoisseurs: Three to Four Years

♥

Sweet Potato and Rosemary Soup

This is a tasty and hearty soup for the whole family. The sweetness of the potatoes balances nicely with the strong aroma and flavor of the rosemary. This soup is perfect for a cold autumn day spent playing indoors.

MAKES 8 SERVINGS

1 large clove garlic, chopped

1 tablespoon olive oil

6 cups vegetable broth

4 cups cubed organic sweet potatoes, about 2 pounds

¼ teaspoon black pepper

¼ teaspoon salt

1 tablespoon finely chopped fresh rosemary

1 cup low-fat milk

In a large pot, sauté garlic in olive oil over medium heat for about 30 seconds. Add broth and potatoes and bring to a boil. Reduce heat to low, cover, and simmer until potatoes are tender, 25 minutes.

Puree soup in batches in a blender until smooth. Be careful as liquid will be hot. Return puree to pot and stir in pepper, salt, rosemary, and milk. Heat over medium heat, stirring, until hot throughout.

KEEPING THEM SWEET

Store sweet potatoes in a dry, cool (55 to 60°F.) place, such as a cellar, pantry, or garage. Do not store them in the refrigerator, where they will develop a hard core and an "off" taste. If stored properly, sweet potatoes will keep for a month or longer.

NUTRITION FACTS

Serving Size: 1 cup (249g)

Calories 100
Calories from Fat 15
Total Fat 2g
Saturated Fat 0g
Cholesterol 0mg
Sodium 610mg
Total Carbohydrate 20g
Dietary Fiber 3g
Sugars 7g
Protein 3g

the
petit
appetit
COOKBOOK
♥

Trail Mix Treat

Trail mix is a great choice for on-the-go snacks or lunch boxes. This is a bit of so-phistication for those who have moved beyond the simple bag of Os.

Choose your child's favorite cereal, fruits, and nuts so the entire mix is eaten.

MAKES 2½ CUPS

1 cup toasted oat or favorite cereal
½ cup organic raisins
½ cup dried organic cranberries
½ cup chopped raw almonds

Mix all ingredients in a bowl. Store in an airtight container at room temperature for up to 2 weeks.

NUTRITION FACTS

Serving Size: about ⅓ cup (30g)

Calories 110
Calories from Fat 35
Total Fat 4g
Saturated Fat 0g
Cholesterol 0mg
Sodium 40mg
Total Carbohydrate 20g
Dietary Fiber 2g
Sugars 12g
Protein 2g

The
Connoisseurs:
Three to Four
Years

♥

Turkey Noodle Soup

It has been estimated that 95 percent of Americans eat turkey at Thanksgiving. Soup is the second most popular way (after sandwiches) to serve leftover turkey. This soup hits the spot for comforting a little (or big) one with a cold.

MAKES 8 SERVINGS

4 cups organic chicken broth

1 small yellow onion, chopped (about ½ cup)

1 medium organic carrot, chopped (about ½ cup)

1 tablespoon minced fresh parsley

½ teaspoon minced fresh thyme

1 bay leaf

½ teaspoon black pepper

4 ounces uncooked macaroni or small pasta shells

2 cups cubed, cooked turkey (about ¾ pound)

1 cup chopped Pomi tomatoes, including juice

In a large pot over medium heat, combine broth, onion, carrot, parsley, thyme, bay leaf, and pepper. Bring to a boil. Stir in macaroni, cover, and reduce heat. Simmer for about 6 minutes. Stir in turkey and tomatoes. Cook until heated through and macaroni is tender. Discard bay leaf before serving.

TURKEYS ON THE MOON?

When Neil Armstrong and Edwin "Buzz" Aldrin sat down to eat their first meal on the moon, their foil food packets contained roasted turkey with all of the trimmings.

Blueberry Muffins and Strawberry Cake

The final two recipes are from Devon and Carolyn, both four-year-olds. They are featured on a placemat of recipes, which I have and had to share, from a company called Bob's Your Uncle. Do not attempt to make these recipes at home . . . maybe at Nana's.

Blueberry Muffins

Blueberry
Sugar
Dough
Salt

Put into muffin things. Put them in the oven. Keep them there for a while. Take out. Eat them.

Strawberry Cake

3 cups of flour
4 eggs
3 cups of oil
5 teaspoons of salt

ICING
1 strawberry and sprinkles

Cook in the oven for 7 hours and 49°F.

Food Introduction Record

When your child begins his culinary adventures it can be difficult to remember which foods your child has tasted and when. Keep a written record to remind yourself and chart any negative reactions. You will want to share this information with your pediatrician if your child has an allergy or illness.

DATE OF INTRODUCTION	FOOD	REACTION/PROBLEM (IF ANY)

DATE OF INTRODUCTION	FOOD	REACTION/PROBLEM (IF ANY)

Appendix A

♥

Toddler Food Diary

Your child's active toddler days may mean more time for playing and less focus on mealtime and eating. If you are not sure how much your child is eating, and are concerned the intake of food is too low, keep a diary of food consumed over a period of a few days, or a week. You may find that all your child's grazing and snacking during the day adds up to a substantial and balanced diet.

This can be a handy tool when preparing and ordering favorite snacks and meals, as well as trying to determine snack times and activities that increase your child's appetite.

Food Diary

DATE	TIME EATEN	AMOUNT/TYPE OF FOOD EATEN	ACTIVITY BEFORE HUNGRY

DATE	TIME EATEN	AMOUNT/TYPE OF FOOD EATEN	ACTIVITY BEFORE HUNGRY

Dippity Doo Da, Dippity Yeah!

Sometimes it's hard to think of creative dips and spreads to excite your children. Don't worry; whether you have an arsenal of dips or none at all, your child will use his imagination and come up with the craziest combinations.

Here are a few fun and easy suggestions that require no measuring or recipes.

Single Item Dips

Cream cheese. Dip raw vegetables such as carrots and celery as well as fruit slices of apples and pears. Also a versatile spread on sandwiches, wraps, and crackers.

Fruit purees, such as apple, peach, and pear. Use for dunking chunks of fruits, pancakes, waffles, and chicken bites.

Mustards. These are very versatile. Honey mustard (do not give honey to babies under 1 year) is of course a favorite for chicken, meatloaf, broccoli, and cauliflower trees. For an Asian flair your child may enjoy mustard with soy sauce for dipping noodles, vegetables, and tofu sticks.

Naturally brewed soy sauce (tamari). Little ones can dunk meats and vegetable chips or pour the sauce over soba and rice dishes.

Organic ketchup. Have on hand for meats, fish sticks, polenta, potato fries, and vegetable chips.

Organic natural nut butters (peanuts are not recommended for children under 2 years). This is pure peanut taste without the trans fats and sugars. Use for dunking cheese sticks, apple slices, graham crackers, and bites of banana.

Vegetable purees, such as avocado, edamame, or spinach. Use as spreads on pitas, tortilla chips, and for dipping vegetable spears.

Yogurt. Serve with angel food cake pieces, toast points, waffles and pancakes, fruits, and vegetables.

Combination Dips

Classic oil and vinegar dressing. Use for dipping pieces of bread or steamed vegetables.

Cottage or ricotta cheese plus any fruit or vegetable puree. Dunk fruit and vegetables pieces, noodles, pancakes, and French toast.

Plain yogurt or cream cheese mixed with spices or herbs. Try yogurt with cinnamon or cream cheese with fresh rosemary or thyme.

Plain yogurt plus any fruit or vegetable puree. Create your own flavors by adding fruit and vegetable purees. Fruit blends work with fruit chunks, vegetables spears, toast points, and waffle pieces. Veggie combos are good for dipping vegetable slices and chicken pieces.

Ideas from Kids

Dip grapes in ketchup.

Dip fingers in mustard.

Dip all food in glass of milk or water.

Tag-Alongs for Movers, Shakers, and Connoisseurs

Here are some quick snacks to bring along for day trips, out for a stroll, or have on hand for school. These snacks are easy to make and don't need a real recipe, only your imagination and your child's appetite.

Remember, vegetables and fruits can make their own snacks with a little extra effort to make them appealing to children. I recommend that moms always carry a fresh avocado and banana in their diaper bag. They are appropriate for all ages, need no refrigeration (until cut), and need no preparation. I have even eaten these healthy staples when in a food bind.

Organic natural peanut butter is a good source of protein and makes a healthy snack paired with the following foods:

- Spread on chunks of apple.

- Spread on toast with a slice of cheddar or Swiss cheese.

- Sandwiched between two waffles or pancakes (page 249).

- Spread on wheat tortilla, topped with a banana rolled up.

Vegetables and fruits can make their own snacks with a little extra effort to make them special and appealing to children.

- Celery stick spread with cream cheese and sprinkled with raisins.

- Zucchini, cut in half lengthwise, spread with Spring Spread (page 166), then put back together.

- A cored apple stuffed with granola or cereal.

- Spinach leaves stuffed with Happy Hummus (page 132) and vegetable sticks and rolled.

- Lettuce leaves stuffed with Happy Days Egg and Olive Spread (page 150) and rolled.

When the bag of toasted oat cereal isn't enough or your child needs variety trail mixes are an easy "to go" snack. Besides the Trail Mix Treat recipe (page 237), here are some other suggestions:

- Handful of toasted oat cereal mixed with raisins.

- Handful of granola (page 193) mixed with dried apricots and cranberries.

- Handful of dried fruit chunks mixed with wheat pretzels.

- Handful of chopped raw almonds mixed with dried fruit chunks.

Pita bread makes a handy and healthy pocket to stuff your child's favorite fillings.

- Stuff with lettuce, avocado, and cheese sticks.

- Stuff with spinach and Happy Hummus (page 132).

- Stuff with Dilly Ricotta Dip (page 118).

- Stuff with leftover meats.

Lavosh or flatbread and tortillas make a neat roll-up for little hands. These rolls can also be cut for a special, colorful presentation, almost like sushi!

- Spread with Roasted Red Pepper Puree (page 176) and vegetable sticks, and roll.

- Spread with Garden Tomato Sauce (page 148), sprinkle with mozzarella cheese, and roll.

- Spread with Baby's Beans (page 95) and sprinkle with jack cheese.

Bagels make a good platform for lots of spread and fillings. Broken into tiny pieces, bagels can be dipped into hummus or goat cheese for young eaters. You can even cut them in half and remove some of the bread, so filling stays in better and the bagel is not so filling for little tummies. Here are a few options:

- Spread with Garden Tomato Sauce (page 148), sprinkle with mozzarella cheese and chopped veggies, like a pizza.

- Stuff with cottage cheese and sliced strawberries.

- Stuff with omelet pieces (page 141).

- Spread with nectarine or other fruit butters (page 117).

Waffles and pancakes can be good for making fun sandwiches and rolls.

- Spread pancakes with cream cheese and any fruit puree and roll up.

- Spread peanut butter and all-fruit spread between two waffles.

- Layer scrambled eggs between waffles for a breakfast sandwich.

Appendix E

Mashies

There are a few fruits and veggies that require little more than a fork and an effort to prepare for your baby. When baby is older, simply cut these favorites into small slices to be eaten by little fingers, or use them to create new flavors and textures for various combinations. Here are a few that do not require cooking or processing.

Baby's Banana

Beginners

Banana combines well with all fruit and vegetable purees, as well as cereal (just like for grown-ups).

1 ripe banana, peeled

Mash banana with a fork. Makes about ¼ to ⅓ cup

Avocado for All Ages

Beginners

Avocado goes well with yogurt or cottage cheese.

1 ripe avocado, peeled and pitted

Mash avocado with a fork. Makes about ¼ to ½ cup

Mango Mash

Beginners

If too tart, mix with pear, apple, or banana purees.

1 mango, peeled and pitted

Mash mango with a fork. Makes about ¼ to ⅓ cup

Kids' Kiwi

Explorers

If too tart, combine with mashed banana or apple puree.

1 ripe kiwifruit, peeled

Mash kiwi with a fork. Makes 3 to 4 tablespoons

Perfectly Papaya

Explorers

Papaya goes well with banana or apricot puree.

1 ripe papaya, peeled and seeded

Mash papaya with a fork. Makes about 1 cup

Melon Madness

Independents
Combine with papaya or apple.

¼ cantaloupe or small seedless watermelon

Dice melon into small pieces. Makes about 1 cup

Berry Good

Independents
Good with kiwi, banana, mango, or fruits purees.

1 handful of strawberries, stems removed

Mash strawberries with a fork. Makes about ¼ cup

Food Information and Shopping Resources

Bob's Red Mill Foods
www.bobsredmill.com

The Gluten-Free Pantry
www.glutenfree.com

CompuFood Analysis
www.compufood.com

Produce Oasis
www.produceoasis.com

Dean and Deluca
www.deananddeluca.com

Trader Joe's
www.traderjoes.com

Food Reference
www.foodreference.com

Whole Foods Market
www.wholefoods.com

Nutrition, Children, and Health Resources

American Academy of Pediatrics
www.aap.org

Celiac Sprue Association
www.csaceliacs.org

BabyCenter
www.babycenter.com

Food and Drug Administration
www.fda.gov

Juvenile Diabetes Research Foundation
www.jdrf.org

Organic Trade Association
www.ota.com

Kids Health
www.kidshealth.org

Web MD
www.webmd.com

Organic Style
www.organicstyle.com

Magazines

Cooking Light
www.cookinglight.com

Parenting
www.parenting.com

Organic Style
www.organicstyle.com

Parents
www.parents.com

Book Resources

Eisenberg, Arlene, Heidi E. Murkoff, and Sandee E. Hathaway, B.S.N. *What to Expect the First Years*. New York: Workman Publishing, 1996.

Gibbs Ostmann, Barbara, and Jane Baker. *The Recipe Writer's Handbook*. New York: John Wiley & Sons, 2001.

Gourmet Magazine, ed. *Gourmet Everyday*. New York: Random House Publishing Group, 2001.

Kimmel, Martha and David, with Suzanne Goldenson. *Mommy Made and Daddy Too: Home Cooking for a Healthy Baby and Toddler*, rev. ed. New York: Bantam Books, 2000.

Knox, Gerald, ed. *Better Homes and Gardens New Cookbook*, 4th ed. Des Moines, IA: *Better Homes and Gardens*, 1989.

Landrigan, Phillip, M.D., Herbert L. Needleman, M.D., and Mary M. Landrigan, M.P.A. *Raising Healthy Children in a Toxic World: 101 Smart Solutions for Every Family*. New York: Rodale Press, 2002.

Lansky, Vicki. *Feed Me I'm Yours*, rev. ed. New York: Meadowbrook Press, 1986.

Roberts, Susan B., Ph.D., and Melvin B. Heyman, M.D., with Lisa Tracy. *Feeding Your Child for Lifelong Health*. New York: Bantam Books, 1999.

Saint Louis Art Museum. *The Artist in the Kitchen*. Saint Louis, MO: The Saint Louis Art Museum, 1993.

Satter, Ellyn. *Child of Mine: Feeding with Love and Good Sense*, 3rd ed. Boulder, CO: Bull Publishing, 2000.

Severson, Kim, with Cindy Burke. *The Trans Fat Solution*. Berkeley, CA: Ten Speed Press, 2003.

Wavrin, Bill. *The Rancho La Puerta Cookbook*. New York: Broadway Books, 1998.

Weil, Andrew, M.D., and Rosie Daley. *The Healthy Kitchen: Recipes for a Better Body, Life, and Spirit*. New York: Alfred A. Knopf, 2002.

Book Resources

Index

Index

♥

Recipe Index

Index

♥

About the Author

Lisa Barnes is the founder of Petit Appetit, a culinary service devoted to the palates and health of infants and toddlers. She started Petit Appetit because she wanted children to have good eating habits and healthy food choices from their very first bite. She believes parents should pay as much attention to their child's palate and dining experiences as they do their own.

Ms. Barnes has worked in a variety of kitchens and classrooms, as well as participated in weekends at the California Culinary Academy. She is a member of the American Personal Chef Association and a Certified Safe Food Handler. In 1999, Lisa contributed to the marketing efforts and recipe testing for the San Francisco Junior League cookbook, *San Francisco Flavors*. She continues to teach in-home private cooking classes to parents, nannies, mothers' groups, and parenting resources throughout Northern California. Her volunteer activities focus on food and community, too. Whether helping cook meals at the Ronald McDonald House or preparing bag lunches at Glide Memorial, Lisa believes food is a great way for people to connect. She believes that kitchens and dining rooms are the heart and soul of a home, where everyone comes to eat, share, laugh, talk, and celebrate. Lisa shares her kitchen and dining room, most importantly, with her husband, Lee, and son, Jonas, in San Francisco.

Her mission is for children to eat more healthfully and for parents to feel empowered to provide tasty and healthy food for their family. Good food should be about nutrition and taste, and bringing the family together.